The World of Motorcycles

AN ILLUSTRATED ENCYCLOPEDIA

COLUMBIA HOUSE/New York

Editor:	Ian Ward
Editorial Director:	Brian Innes
Assistant Editors:	Laurie Caddell
	Brian Laban
	Mike Winfield
Editorial Assistants:	Jenny Dawson
	David Vivian
Art Editors:	David Goodman
	Andrew Weall
Designer:	Sue Horner
Picture:	Mirco Decet
Picture Researcher:	Clive Gorman
Cover Photo:	Warner Brothers;
	Hillelson Library
Design:	Harry W. Fass
Production:	Stephen Charkow

Contributors:
GEOFF ADAMS: Learning
ALAN BAKER: Kickstart
ROY BUCHANAN: Jonsson
LAURIE CADDELL:
    Kawasaki Z1000, Z650, KH125
    Laverda 500 and Jota
PETER CARRICK: Karsmakers
    Kawasaki
    Kreidler
PETER CLIFFORD: Lawwill
ANDREW EDWARDS: Jancarz
    Jessup
FRANK GLENDINNING: James
    JAP
PETER HOWDLE: Lampkin

DOUG JACKSON: Lambretta
CHRISTOPHER JAMES:
    Italian Grand Prix
    Jarama
PETER KELLY: Isle of Man
    Kanaya
    Lansivuori
PHIL MATHER: Knievel
ANDREW McKINNON: Katayama
DAVE MINTON: Italjet
RICHARD PLATT: Levis
L.J.K. SETRIGHT: Laverda
MIKE WINFIELD: Italjet CX80R
    KTM 250
    Lambretta GP150
    Van Veen OCR 1000
ALAN WRAIGHT: KTM

Picture acknowledgments
Page 841: D. Morley—842: A. Morland—843–4: A. Morland—845: B. Jackson; A. Morland—846: B. Jackson; A. Morland—847: Publifoto—848–9: Publifoto; LAT—850: LAT; Keystone—851: Popperfoto—852: LAT—853: D. Minton—854: Italjet—855: D. Vinton; Italjet—856: D. Jackson—857: D. Minton; D. Jackson—858: D. Minton—859–60: J. Spencer Smith/Orbis—861: E. Thompson—862: R. Bonson—863: National Motor Museum—864–5: Motor Cycle—866: T. Meeks—867: T. Meeks—868–9: Motor Cycle—870: J. Spencer Smith/Orbis—871–4: J. Heese—875–6:

T. Meeks—877: J. Heese—878: J. Greening; J. Heese—879–80: J. Heese—881: J. Heese—882: J. Heese—883: L. J. Caddell/Orbis—884: L. J. Caddell/Orbis—885: J. Heese—886: D. Jackson; J. Heese—887: Le Moto—888: D. Jackson; Kawasaki—889: J. Spencer Smith/Orbis; Le Moto—890–1: J. Heese—893: J. Heese; A. McGuire—894: All-sport—895: I. Ward—896: I. Ward—897: M. Decet—898: L. J. Caddell—899: J. Spencer Smith/Orbis—900: J. Spencer Smith/Orbis—901: Kawasaki; I. Dawson/Orbis—902: J. Spencer Smith/Orbis—903: J. Spencer Smith/Orbis; B. Mayor—904: Warner Brothers—905–6: Cycle News—907: L. Parkins; T. Duffy—908–9: Hillelson library—910: Warner Brothers—911: Kreidler—912: J. Heese; D. Jackson—913: D. Jackson; J. Heese—914–5–6–7: J. Heese—918: J. Heese; D. Jackson—919: J. Heese; D. Jackson—920: J. Heese; D. Jackson—921: J. Spencer Smith/Orbis—922: J. Spencer Smith/Orbis—923: National Motor Museum—924: Motor Cycle—925: Cycle Trader; Lambretta—926: D. Jackson; National Motor Museum—927: L. J. Caddell/Orbis—928: L. J. Caddell/Orbis—929, 930, 931, 932: N. Nicholls—933: J. Heese—934: J. Greening; J. Heese—935: D. Jackson—936: D. Jackson—937: D. Jackson; Laverda—938: R. Adams; J. Greening—939: J. Heese; D. Morley—940: Laverda; L. J. Caddell; J. Heese—941: J. Greening—942: J. Heese—943, 944, 945, 946: L. J. Caddell/Orbis—947: M. Woollett—948: R. Adams; J. Stoddart—949: L. J. Caddell/Orbis—950: B. Mayor/Orbis—951, 952, 953, 954: L. J. Caddell/Orbis—955, 956: R. Platt/VMCC—957: Motor Cycle; L. J. Caddell/Orbis—958: VMCC—959: VMCC; T. Stimpson/Orbis—960: VMCC

Contents   Page

The Island

Slowly, the excited chatter in the Grandstand dies down and all is silent – so deadly silent – in anticipation of that first patter of feet, that first sound of racing engines firing up and rising to a blood-curdling crescendo as the first two riders leap aboard their machines and scream down Bray Hill at the start of the Isle of Man TT.

The 37¾-mile Mountain circuit is pure magic to the enthusiast. The toughest, greatest road race in the world. There will never be another like it.

The TT started in 1907, but racing was not always over the 'Mountain'. The first race set off from St John's, on the Douglas to Peel road, and much later there was also the Clypse circuit for smaller bikes and sidecars.

By 1977 there was only one TT circuit, rising steeply from Ramsey, over bleak mountain roads which reach a height of 1300 feet and more at Brandywell, and it is over this circuit that we shall take our trip.

It starts at the Grandstand, on the Glencrutchery Road, a steep climb from Douglas promenade. This is the nerve-centre of the event. Opposite the Grandstand is one of the world's most intricate leaderboards, recording the position and lap of every single rider. At each end of this giant display, and also beneath the Dunlop clock in the centre, are special boards recording the first six riders on each lap, their lap times, speeds and averages. These are painted on immediately the times become known.

Between these big displays is a 'clock' for every single rider in the race. It has three main positions – for Glen Helen, Ramsey and the Bungalow, and as each rider reaches these points on the course the fingers are moved around accordingly by hordes of busy boy scouts.

Beneath the Grandstand are the pits, and each rider's attendants wait there with all the necessary tools and spare parts. There is a petrol gravity fill tank for every single rider.

Left: Kate's Cottage is one of the best known landmarks of the TT course. The very exacting nature of this most difficult of road circuits makes it the ultimate challenge in the history of motor cycle racing

The riders set off in pairs at ten-second intervals. The first pair come to the line, the flag marshal looks at his watch, a small flag drops and they are away – on that spine-chilling plunge under the Dunlop bridge and down Bray Hill. Lines of suburban houses flash by as the riders take the right-hand kink down the hill. Then comes the suspension-bottoming crump at the bottom of Bray before the road rises slightly and riders begin to set their machines up, braking heavily, for Quarter Bridge.

Quarter Bridge is a traffic island for ordinary road users, but TT riders go to the right of this and heel over sharp right, heading now along the Peel road, past the remains of the old Isle of Man Steam Railway on the left, along a smooth and straight road.

Within a quarter of a mile comes Braddan Bridge, a vicious 'S' bend approached by a right-hander under the shade of trees. The corner itself goes left then right. The railway used to go under the road here, and there is also a gurgling stream. On the left of the bend stands Kirk Braddan, and in front of it, on a large sloping lawn, are hundreds of seats for spectators. After this, riders lean inwards to avoid a jutting-out wall, and over a slight rise towards Union Mills.

The downhill approach to this little Manx village is to the right and the left, past the Railway Inn on the left, and a post office on the right. Walls are well straw-baled at both sides of this, one of the most notorious parts of the circuit.

The road then goes left again and up a long, straight hill towards Crosby, a ribbon development suburb of Douglas made up mostly of semi-detached houses. The approach is uphill but nevertheless very fast. The Crosby Hotel, standing on the right, is a favourite venue for spectators.

Emerging again into open countryside, with hills to the right and left, the course goes downhill again for the flat-out blind past the famous Highlander Inn, chosen for many years by time-trap operators as it was thought that this was the fastest part of the course. Whether this is still true is disputable, for the sheer speed of modern bikes means that riders are thinking of braking for the right- and left-hand flick which follows just before the Sixth Milestone.

Next, past whitewashed little cottages with flower gardens spilling out on to the footpath, comes Appledene, a tight left and right with trees overhanging each side of the circuit. After another right-hand corner with a distinctive little cottage on the left comes the fast left-hander of Greeba Bridge, then it's fairly straight, past the famous

Hawthorne Inn on the left, to Ballacraine.

At Ballacraine, the TT course turns off the Peel road and to the right, past the front of the Ballacraine Hotel, and on through Ballaspur into one of the slowest and most difficult parts of the circuit, towards Glen Helen. Here, corners are too numerous to mention, but are all deadly to the inexperienced. This particular section of the course has been greatly improved by resurfacing work in recent years, and as a result is much quicker than in the spine-shaking days of old. The one that stands out is Laurel Bank. With a left-hand approach, it is a very tight right-hander and here many riders – both in racing

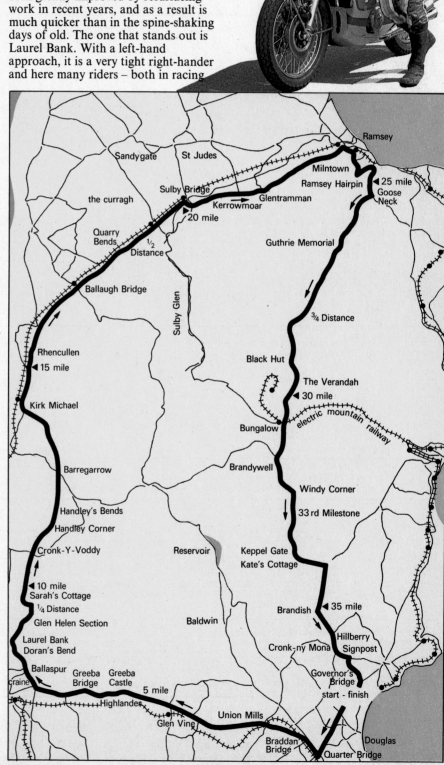

Left: only a few seconds to go as this rider prepares to start on a lap of the Isle of Man course. As the flag drops he will gun his machine into life, accelerate along the start and finish straight and then set off on the terrifying descent of Bray Hill

Below: rounding Quarter Bridge; it is normally a traffic island for ordinary road users, but the TT riders go to the right of this. Heeling over sharp right the riders then head along the Peel Road, past the remains of the old Isle of Man Steam Railway on the left, on a road which is relatively smooth and straight, then on towards the vicious and tricky 'S' bend at Braddan Bridge

and on the road – have taken nasty spills. This part is also noticeable especially in June for the overwhelming smell of wild garlic.

The Ninth Milestone, a sharp left-hander with a right-hand exit, leads to Glen Helen itself, one of the most beautiful points on the course. Through sun-dappled shades filled with birdsong, it is a tight left, then right, then left again – a tricky one – uphill to Sarah's Cottage. Once a tiny rustic dwelling on the left, Sarah's Cottage has been replaced by a bigger house. The road continues uphill through a tight right-hander and now the road changes from smooth tarmacadam to a rough, undulating surface which is cruel on

frames, suspension and exhaust mountings. Along this section, bikes leap from the road and come down with bone-shaking jolts, over crossroads with a small, old church on the right. Then it twists downwards towards the Eleventh Milestone, a better surface again, and on to Handley's Corner, named after the great Wal, who came a cropper there in the dim and distant past.

Handley's is a left- and right-handed flick with a high stone wall and cottage on the right. The next section is tricky, too, past the Twelfth Milestone and on towards the frightening section through Barregarrow. The bottom of Barregarrow has always been one for

sorting the men from the boys. To see a top-class rider plunge down the steep hill, his machine bouncing about alarmingly, and to hear him keep the throttle open over a little white-painted bridge and a sharp left-hander, coming frighteningly close to a jutting-out wall of a white house, is a thrilling experience.

Past the Thirteenth Milestone, the road goes through a long, sweeping right-hander, then left and left again in a sharp double bend and on to the straight towards the village of Kirk Michael. Just before the village street, and pointed out by a large red arrow, is a tight, wide right-hand corner which brings the speeds right down. Then the bikes scream headlong through the narrow village streets, the noise echoing against the walls of shops and houses. The road goes straight on, past a garage on the left, and through yet another series of bends before it opens out widely, with a smooth surface, along an avenue of trees for the fast approach to Ballaugh Bridge.

The white-painted iron railings of Ballaugh Bridge must be one of the most familiar sights on TT photographs. The only humpback bridge left on the TT course – there used to be half a dozen or more – it goes at an angle across a stream. Riders decelerate rapidly, line up for the left-hand approach with a notoriously difficult exit dead in line with house walls, leave the road for a moment, then come down with a crump and bear hard right and left out of the village, past the Raven's Nest pub, another favourite of TT supporters.

After Ballaugh, the course goes on past forested mountains on the right, along a straight but bumpy stretch of road towards the Mooragh Wildlife Park and Quarry Bends. A series of tricky corners in the gloom of overhanging trees, the Quarries can be taken incredibly quickly by experienced riders. From here, it goes on through a fast left kink, over the Sulby Crossroads and on to the now extremely rough-riding Sulby Straight. This was once thought to be the fastest part of the circuit, but suspension now takes such a hammering here, with riders often on the verge of losing control, that it is unlikely still to be the case.

There is a right-hand kink past rows of cottages before the awesome right-hander of Sulby Bridge is reached. Here the course completely changes direction again and heads towards Ramsey, going hard left and left again past the famous Ginger Hall hotel on the right.

Next comes Kerrowmoar, an ultra-tricky left-hander leading into a right-handed flick, and from here to Ramsey

Above: because the TT course is a real road circuit, visitors to the Isle of Man can tackle the track for themselves when it is not closed for racing. Here a group of riders round Ramsey Hairpin

Left: two sidecar outfits flash through Laurel Bank

Below: as a BMW sweeps round Creg-ny-Baa, Kate's Cottage can be seen in the background. By the time a rider reaches Creg-ny-Baa, he has completed almost 35 miles of the track

there are so many corners that a rider's full attention is required. Heeling over to left and right, changing gear continuously, beneath the trees of Glen Tramman and past the 22nd Milestone, he cannot let up for one moment.

The road straightens out a little on the approach to Milntown Cottage, a small, whitewashed house on the left, with forested trees on the right. Soon, riders take the left-handed School House Corner, now resurfaced, and enter the 30mph environs of Ramsey – but they take no notice of the official road signs as the road narrows between houses towards the town centre and Parliament Square.

At Parliament Square, riders heel sharp right across a halt sign, then hard left, beneath a footbridge, up May Hill. A sharp uphill right-hander, with a hump in the road that can produce sensational wheelies, leads, increasingly steeply, to the Ramsey Hairpin, a popular spectator spot where all kinds of different lines are attempted, clutch slipping, as riders coax their bikes round the ultra-sharp, climbing left-hand hairpin. Then the road bears right, and right again at Waterworks Corner. If riders could spare the time they would see a magnificent view of Ramsey Bay spread out below.

It's all uphill now, heading towards the Mountain section where spectators have uninterrupted views of miles of road. Past the 25th Milestone and on towards the Gooseneck, a left followed by a right. On a clear day, parts of Scotland and Northern Ireland can be seen from here. The next point on the mountain climb is Guthrie's Memorial. The surface improves again as Guthrie's is approached. A sweeping left- and right-hander, the road crosses a small stone bridge and on the right is the memorial stone itself – in honour of the great Jimmy Guthrie, of Hawick, who died 'while upholding the honour of his country in the German Grand Prix, August 1937'.

From Guthrie's the TT course continues to climb, bordered by sheep fences on each side. This is three-quarter distance and, apart from the occasional bend, is flat-out for much of the way. Then comes the series of left-handers, which riders try to treat as one long corner, at Mountain Box. By now, the gales which often sweep in from the sea can be felt by the battling TT men. The road is now wider, with chamfered kerbstones, as it leads towards Black Hut, a continuous left-hander, then a right, close to the spot where Italian rider Gilberto Parlotti was killed in fog, and which led to many top riders deciding to boycott the race until improvements were made to the course. The road now levels off, then heads downhill to Bungalow Bridge and the Bungalow, right, left and right, over the tracks of the Snaefell Mountain Railway from Laxey. Here, there is ample parking space and refreshments for spectators. There is a Manx Radio commentary point on the left, and it is here that the TT Rescue helicopter is normally stationed.

The climb then continues past fenced-in moorland to Brandywell, the highest point of the course, where the road goes to the right and left before the downhill plunge to Windy Corner, a

845

very tight right-hander where a vicious wind normally blows in between the mountains from the Irish Sea. From here it's all downhill, and very bumpy, to the 33rd Milestone, a double left-hander, and then through Keppel Gate, where the road goes to the right and the left before steepening into the tight left-hander of Kate's Cottage, a farmhouse to the right of the road.

Now comes the stomach-turning drop, straight downhill on a bumpy road that's like a series of steps, to the Keppel Hotel at the bottom and the right-hand bend at Creg-ny-Baa, where John Williams came to grief on a works Suzuki four in the 1977 Open Classic event.

The Creg itself, with each side of the road linked by a footbridge, is usually crammed with spectators and coach parties. They can see the bikes dropping from Kate's, then braking heavily for the bend, and flying on downhill on a much smoother surface towards Brandish Corner. On this section of really narrow road, Yorkshireman Mick Grant hit an astonishing 191mph on the works 750cc three-cylinder Kawasaki when he won the six-lap

Classic, at an average of over 110mph.

It's a billiard-table surface now, as riders approach the tight left-hander, bordered by white-painted railings, at Brandish, then get flat-out again on another long downhill straight to Hillberry. Here, the road hits a dip and climbs again, and is hard on suspensions as riders get well over to the right of the track for this right-hander, followed by a left and then the ultra-steep right-hand turn of Signpost Corner.

The race is almost over now – or at least one lap of it. At Signpost, a message is flashed to the leaderboard as each rider goes through, and a bulb lights up to warn the pit crews to get ready. Although the start-finish line is in their grasp, many fine men have lost it on the tricky, bumpy, evil little sections of road between here and Governor's Bridge. Governor's is a double hairpin, going to both right and left, with an adverse camber. Clutches which have almost given up the ghost have been known to break for good here as riders struggle out on to the main road to the right once more and open up for the final, straight, quarter-mile dash to the chequered flag.

Well, that's a quick run-down of the longest road circuit in the world. If it seems a long, long way, it is sobering to note that a rider like Mick Grant took exactly 20 minutes and four seconds in 1977 to get round, at an average speed in excess of 112mph and even then it seemed that the 20-minute race barrier would be broken before too long.   PK

Below: the very tight Governor's Bridge hairpin from both sides. As the machines come out of the darkness, they have a very tight right-hander to negotiate. Luckily, as the corner is at a crossroads, there is ample run-off area. Naturally, when in competition, the riders take no notice at all of the signs in the road!

The Italian Grand Prix has a long and chequered history stretching back to 1922. The first, in September 1922 was held on the then new Monza circuit near Milan.

The circuit was 6¾ miles long, and consisted of a smaller oval circuit inside a larger roughly oval track. Two races were run, a 1000cc event won by Italian rider Ruggeri on a Harley Davidson, who completed the 248½ miles at an average speed of 64.8mph, while the 500cc race, in the afternoon, over the same distance, was another Italian, Gnesa, riding a Garelli.

Monza continued to stage races for ten years, and so popular was the event – with both spectators and competitors, that the programme grew to include 125, 175, 250, 350 and 500cc races.

In 1933 the Circuito del Littorio in Rome staged the GP, and though the event stayed there for another season, it was back to Monza in 1935, and there it remained until the outbreak of war in 1939. When the FICM, the governing body of motor cycle sport at that time decided to introduce the European Championship, the Italian was one of eight major meetings that counted towards the title.

The race had a good cross section of nationalities in both men and machines. Britain's Ted Mellors won the 350cc race on a Velocette, while Georg Meier of Germany thrashed his BMW round the Monza banking at 157.136kph, and Italian Soprani on a Benelli grabbed the 250cc honours.

The Italian factories were a force to be reckoned with once racing resumed, and in the Italian GP of 1947, run at the Circuito della Fiera in Milan, Gilera won the 500cc event, thanks to Artesani, and Moto Guzzi took the 250cc class.

For 1948, the race switched to the short Circuito di Faenza, but as it clashed with the International Six Days trial and the Manx GP in the Isle of Man, British factories were busy elsewhere. The Italian factories had little opposition. In the 500cc race Masserini on a four-cylinder Gilera beat Lorenzetti on the works single-cylinder Moto Guzzi, who had earlier that season won the Ulster GP.

Bertoni, on an MV won the 125cc race, with Ruffo's Moto Guzzi second, but the meeting was not a great success, and so for 1949 the races switched back to Monza, and the start of the new world championships! The circuit now measured 6.3 kilometres.

Les Graham on the new AJS Porcupine was in tremendous form in 1949, and thanks to wins at the Swiss GP and Ulster GP, and a second at the Dutch he won the first ever 500cc crown, but he was out of luck at Monza.

Fighting for the lead with Carlo Bandirola, on the works Gilera, the Italian crashed, and his machine brought down Graham too, leaving Nello Pagani victory on another Gilera.

Ambrosini on the Benelli won the 250cc race, and for the first time a sidecar class was included in the event, won by another Italian, Frigerio, on a Gilera.

The Italians had a shock in store at the 1950 GP, when Englishman Geoff

Above: the start of the Italian 500cc Grand Prix of 1959 held at Monza. The race was an MV-Agusta benefit with John Surtees winning from team-mate Remo Venturi. In third place came the legendary Geoff Duke mounted on a Norton, his Gilera days a thing of the past

Duke on the factory Norton won the 350 and 500cc races against the best in the world.

In the sidecar race that year another Englishman, Eric Oliver, who had managed only a fifth the previous season, showed the way round when he won at record breaking speed to clinch the sidecar title for the second successive year.

The Italians fared better in 1951. Again the race was held at Monza, and Carlo Ubbiali on a Mondial won the 125cc race to win the world championship.

Lorenzetti, on a Guzzi grabbed the 250cc honours, Alfredo Milani won the 500cc race for Gilera, with his teammates Umberto Masetti and Nello Pagani in second and third place, and another Milani, Albino, beat Eric Oliver and Pip Harris to take victory in the sidecar event.

Geoff Duke, pushed into fourth position in the 500cc event had the consolation of winning the 350cc from Ken Kavanagh and Jack Brett.

From 1952 until 1965, British or colonial riders won the 500cc race at the Italian GP every year, except twice!

Les Graham, Geoff Duke, John Surtees, Gary Hocking and Mike Hailwood were the men who dominated the class on MV Agusta or Gilera, though Umberto Masetti on an MV grabbed a win in 1955 and Libero Liberatti on a Gilera was the winner in 1957.

But it wasn't just the 500cc class that saw Italian factories dominating. The 350cc Moto Guzzi was an impressive device too. Fergus Anderson and Dickie Dale won the 350cc class at the Italian GPs in 1954 and 55.

Top speed racing, national success and exciting action were the keynotes of the Monza circuit, but as a viewing spectacle, it left much to be desired, even though the length was cut to 5.780 kilometres in 1954. In the 60s the crowds began to dwindle and from a financial consideration as much as anything else it was decided to switch the GP to the 5 kilometre Circuito del Santerno in Imola.

Imola staged its first Grand Prix in 1969 bringing to an end the Monza monopoly of the race which had stretched back, unbroken for 20 years. Some people were not so pleased at the move, though. Count Agusta, head of

the MV factory, was furious that the race had been moved off his doorstep, and so he refused to let Giacomo Agostini or the MV machines race there!

There was no Italian domination this time, though. Dutchman Paul Lodewijkx on the home-built Jamathi won the 50cc race, and Dave Simmonds, who had already clinched the 125cc title, won the 125cc race on his rapid Kawasaki, beating Lazlo Szabo the Hungarian, on the works MZ, and the Villa brothers Francesco and Walter on their home-made machines.

Phil Read asked Benelli to lend him a machine for this meeting. The company refused, so Phil raced his own Yamaha, and won the 250cc race from Australian Kel Carruthers on a Benelli!

Phil won the 350cc race, beating the incredible Silvio Grassetti who was on a works Jawa, despite stopping in the pits for 20 seconds to sort out a loose exhaust pipe.

The 500cc race was won by Alberto Pagani, son of Nello Pagani who had won the same class 20 years earlier at Monza. Pagani was riding a Linto, and it looked for a while as if the little

Right: Steve Baker (Yamaha) leads Pat Hennen and Wil Hartog (Suzukis) during the 1977 Italian 500cc Grand Prix held at Imola. Neither Hennen nor Hartog finished, but Baker was finally placed fourth. The race was won by Britain's Barry Sheene, on the works Texaco Heron Suzuki RGA500, who was to go on and clinch his second World Championship later in the season at Imatra in Finland

Below: Monza, near Milan, has, with only a few exceptions, been the home of the Italian Grand Prix. This is the start of the 350cc Grand Prix of Nations held at Monza in September 1956. Among the riders are Bill Lomas (Moto Guzzi, 12) and Geoff Duke, riding the works Gilera four (number two)

factory might take first and second places, but the machine ridden by Australian John Dodds developed a misfire and he dropped back to third spot, letting Gilberto Milani into a runner up position.

The race was back to Monza the following year. Count Agusta was happy again, and Giacomo Agostini won the 350 and 500cc races on a pair of MVs.

Rod Gould won the 250cc race from Kel Carruthers to win the 250cc world title, Dutchman Jan de Vries took the 50cc honours on the Van Veen Kreidler, and Angel Nieto won the 125cc event.

Monza staged the 1971 Italian GP, too, and again, little Jan de Vries proved quickest of the 50s. But an Italian, Gilbert Parlotti, tragically killed later in the 1972 Isle of Man TT races, took the 125cc class on the new Morbidelli. Giacomo Agostini won the 350cc world title that year, but sometimes things didn't always go his way. A young Finn, Jarno Saarinen had

arrived and on his own privately entered Yamaha, won both the Czech and Italian 350cc races.

Gyula Marsovsky, an Hungarian who had fled to Switzerland after the uprising in his country, won the 250cc race, and Alberto Pagani, now a member of the MV team scored his second GP success; he was first in the 500cc race.

The GP was back to Imola in 1972, and the crowds flocked to the town to watch the meeting. There was action on and off the track because after the 50cc race had ended with Dutchman Jan de Vries beating Spaniard Angel

Nieto over the line, a minor skirmish between Nieto and another Dutchman, Jan Huberts, right in front of the main grandstand had the crowd on their feet.

The 250cc race was superb too, with Italian Renzo Pasolini beating Rod Gould and eventual world champion Jarno Saarinen to the line. Pasolini chased Ago home in the 350cc race, with Saarinen third, but life was easier for Ago in the 500cc event, where he headed home his team-mate Alberto Pagani for a very comfortable win.

The blackest year for the Italian GP was without doubt 1973. The world

championship round was run at Monza and after a thrilling 350cc race won by Giacomo Agostini from Finn Teuvo Lansivuori and Swede Kent Andersson, the 250cc race began.

At the Grand Curve, soon after the start, a multiple pile-up saw many riders injured and both Finn Jarno Saarinen and Italian Renzo Pasolini killed.

The meeting was abandoned, and despite an attempt to improve the safety facilities at Monza in 1977, attempts to run the GP at Monza since then, have been blocked by competitors who have become much more conscious of safety

Top left: Carlo Ubbiali's 125cc
MV-Agusta finished third at Monza in
1954

Top right: Barry Sheene celebrates his
500cc win at Imola in 1977

Above left: the 500cc machines line up at
Imola prior to the start of the 1977
Italian Grand Prix

Above right: Luigi Taveri (125 Honda)
at Monza in 1963

Right: Walter Villa in trouble in 1964

requirements.

Imola ran the GP in 1974 and '75, with two chicanes added for safety reasons, but there were one or two dramatic moments then as well. A move by the Yamaha and Suzuki factories in '74, for example, to cut the race distance in the 500cc event was squashed by the chief of police after hearing that MV would pull out if the race was shortened. He feared a riot.

In the race, Giacomo Agostini, who had switched that season from MV Agusta to Yamaha ran out of petrol when leading, giving newcomer Franco Bonera his first GP success on the MV.

Earlier though, Ago won the 350cc race on his new Yamaha, beating a talented Italian youngster, Mario Lega, and in the 250cc class that year, Walter Villa won on the Harley Davidson helping him on to victory in the world championship.

There was a sidecar race at Imola that year won by Klaus Enders, but the following season the crowd overjoyed that Giacomo Agostini on the Yamaha had beaten Phil Read on the MV, surged on to the track, and the police were unable to control the situation.

The three wheeler race was cancelled, and it hasn't been included in the Italian GP since that time.

The sad episode showed two things, firstly that the Italians were not so keen on sidecar racing, and secondly, just how rapidly the interest in motor cycle racing had grown in Europe. Just six years earlier, the crowd at Imola had been around 30,000. In 1975 it had grown to almost four times that number.

That 1975 Italian GP was another history making meeting, for it saw the arrival in Europe of young Venezuelan Johnny Cecotto. The youngster, of Italian descent, was popular with the Imola crowd and when he beat Ago in the 350cc race they went wild! But Walter Villa was able to inflict a defeat on Cecotto in the 250cc class.

The 1976 Italian GP was switched to another new circuit at Mugello, and though the racing was good, there was a staggering number of crashes with two fatalities. Otello Buscherini and Paolo Tordi, both Italians, died in separate accidents in the 250 and 350cc races, and the anticipated crowd of 60,000 was more like only half that figure.

The 500cc race was perhaps the most

memorable part of the day's entertainment, where Barry Sheene snatched a slender victory over Phil Read on the line after a race-long scrap.

Cecotto beat newcomer Franco Uncini in the 350cc race, and Walter Villa on the Harley Davidson was first with Takazumi Katayama second in the 250cc event.

It was back to Imola for the 1977 Italian GP and the crowd once again rocketed to near 100,000. The meeting and venue may be popular with the fans and riders, but the organisers of the superb Imola 200 mile race earlier in the year find the GP an embarrassment and a strain on their resources.   CJ

Below: Eugenio Lazzarini and his Van Veen Kreidler on their way to victory in the 1977 Italian 50cc Grand Prix at Imola. The 50cc race proved to be very exciting, with Lazzarini coming from behind to win, much to the delight of his fellow countrymen. In second and third positions came Bultaco team-mates Ricardo Tormo and Angel Nieto. Fastest lap was set by Herbert Rittberger (Kreidler) at the quite remarkable speed of 79.85mph

Child's play

The likelihood that anyone believed there was a fortune to be made from manufacturing miniature motor cycles a few years ago is pretty remote, yet this is exactly what Italjet have succeeded in doing. A few full sized machines have been produced, but the bulk of the company business interests have been concentrated on the development and construction of children's motor cycles.

When he started his motor cycle manufacturing concern in 1957, Leopoldo Tartarini had little idea where it would lead, but an ever increasing number of requests from motor cycling parents for specially tailored childrens' machines led him eventually to installing a 'schoolboy' scrambler production line shortly after 1959. Without any shadow of doubt this was as much due to his family background as to his business interests.

'Leo' Tartarini was born on 10 August 1932, the son of Egisto Tartarini who was himself an Italian road racer of renown during the 'thirties. Right from the start Leo's destiny was mapped out for him, his whole life being centred on anything with an engine in it. In the late 'thirties, for instance, the young lad made a name for himself in the Italian press by flying a miniature aircraft designed and built by his father, although as a safety precaution it was tethered to a stake, around which it buzzed. Another 'toy' was a pint sized sidecar outfit, which

Below: no, this is not the start of a world motocross championship event, but a view of the schoolboy scrambling scene in which Italjet is so prominent

probably sowed the seeds of enthusiasm for child sized machinery in the impressionable young Tartarini.

With family friends such as Omobo Tenni, Giordino Aldrighetti, and Guglielmo Sandri, ace works road racers every one, it was not surprising that, despite remarkable academic achievements in science at the Bologna University, Leo found himself becoming inextricably involved with motor cycling.

In 1952, the 20-year-old Tartarini bought himself a secondhand BSA A10 (650 twin) power unit around which he wrapped a rolling chassis designed and built entirely by himself. With a sidecar attached he won the 900-mile Milano-Taranto road race three wheeler class and became a national hero overnight. The following year Leo had achieved fame enough to have his entry accepted in the solo classes of the Giro d'Italia (Tour of Italy) on a 125 Benelli, though at that time such events were heavily oversubscribed. In an entry of over 400, including all the premier aces of Italy, Leo won outright, beating even the 'big' 175s.

That same year he came third overall to a couple of works riders on 500 Gileras in the Milan-Taranto race solo classes, and won the 125 class. In 1954 he won the Giro d'Italia outright again. Needless to say, Leopoldo's Benelli, by that time, owed much more to Tartarini than it did to its original designer, being little more than a Tartarini rolling chassis, around a Tartarini tuned and improved Benelli power unit.

Right up to 1957 Leo kept on racing and winning in all motor cycling classes of long distance road racing, including a win at the city streets circuit of Montjuich (Barcelona) in Spain, but then he found himself being swamped by requests from other riders to either build or improve their machinery. In 1959 he gave in and turned his hand to the serious business of commercial frame building. Italjet was under way.

By this time Egisto Tartarini had died, tragically killed in a racing accident, so Leo took over the family business completely. Situated in Bologna, close to the Appennine hills of northern Italy, the Tartarini empire was founded in farming and the Citroën concession for Italy. During the 'sixties the Italjet factory was built at the little town of San Lazzaro, six kilometres outside Bologna. Since then the influence of Italjet has spread into many other spheres, although all of them are within the automotive industry.

Some of the most famous models of Italian prestige sports cars have been styled by Tartarini, but perhaps the most famous name to be connected with Italjet over the past few years, at least as far as motor cyclists are concerned, is that of Ducati.

When Taglioni, Ducati's engineering chief, finished his part in the design of the vee-twins, Tartarini was called in to style them. Unfortunately all too few, if any, photographic records remain of the pre-production vee-twins, but they were displayed at the Milan show of 1973. A diluted memory of the styling lingered on in the later vee-twins, although they became fat, bulging things compared to the sleek, if radical, lines of the originals, in which the line of the fixed headlamp nacelle flowed handsomely with the fuel tank and side panels to make an extremely attractive motor cycle.

Even more recently, the two companies have co-operated in the production of the Ducati 500 parallel twin. Ducati have been unprofitable for more years than anyone connected with them cares to remember, and are state owned, the motor cycle division being subordinate to the stationary engine division which does make money. Not surprisingly the latter's requirements take precedence, so its expansion left little room for the installation of the 500 twin production line. The problem was finally resolved with Ducati manufacturing the power unit, and then sending it on to Italjet – just three and a half miles down

Opposite page: Italjet believe in catching them young; this young gentleman was already a master of his Mini Bambino at the age of four

Above: among Italjet's large 1977 range were the Mini Bambino, the competition Junior Cross CX50S and the CX80R racer

Below: Leo Tartarini, seen here in 1936, also started riding at a very tender age; perhaps this explains his enthusiasm for building children's bikes

the road – who installed it into the rolling chassis that they designed and manufactured in its entirety.

Apart from motor cycles, dune buggies, snowmobiles and various other associated leisure and sport vehicles are made, but childrens' machines are Italjet's focal point of interest and commercial success.

The range starts with a diminutive motor cycle, the Mini Mini Bambino MM5B, a sub-miniature equipped with eight inch wheels in order that three-year-olds might enjoy a safe and secure start in motor cycling. The Franco Morini (as opposed to Moto Morini) two-stroke power unit is equipped with a single gear and an automatic clutch to make things as simple as possible for the toddlers, and the engine turns out a gentle 1.3bhp on a compression ratio of 6.5:1. The bike weighs a mere 57lb. An almost identical machine is offered with 10inch wheels to enable parents to uprate the machines inexpensively as their children grow and require more leg room.

First of the proper motor cycles, although still of the child sized type, is the Junior Cross Automatic JC5B which, by 1977, had undergone considerable improvement in order to maintain its place at the head of the pack in the six to eight year old noviciate class of schoolboy scrambling, in the Cadet division. The limit here was 50cc, so the JC5B's Franco Morini power unit turned out a rorty 5.5bhp at 8000rpm, again on only one gear and an automatic clutch. In all other respects it was a pukka bike, however, as schoolboy scramble organizers felt that youngsters up to eight years old already had quite enough to cope with without the need for gearchanging as well. The bike weighed in at 81lb.

For the more experienced lads (and girls, in the day and age of female liberation) there were a couple of real racers, these bikes being the over-the-counter Junior Cross Super Competition CX50, complete with a four-speed gearbox, and the competition shop built Grand Prix CX50R. The former produced 5bhp at 8500rpm from its Minarelli engine on a compression ratio of 9.5:1, while the latter turned out 5.5bhp at 9000rpm on a compression ratio of 11:1 and a special alloy barrel with fiercer port timing. The CX50R also boasted competition quality suspension with two way damping and larger, more powerful brakes, plus numerous other extras. Significantly, all models were equipped with steel rims to deal with the hammering the children handed out.

Above: Italjet's Piranha was built for the ISDT and used a 100cc Jawa engine developing 11.4 bhp at 8500rpm

Right: a 1973 single-cylinder Minarelli engined Italjet 125

Still in the Junior class of schoolboy scrambling were the 80cc machines on which the aces of the age group competed. In this instance only one model was offered in 1977 because by this time youngsters had developed into skillful riders knowing all too well the necessity of competitive machinery at its absolute best. This machine was the CX80R, a scaled down replica of a full blooded, king sized, adult scrambler churning out 13bhp at 10,500rpm on a compression ratio of 13:1. The interesting thing about this machine lay in its engine. Although this was a Minarelli, the unit was one of strictly limited production, and came from the competition shop of the factory, each one being hand built from selected components. Only eight a day were built, and all specially for Italjet. Gas filled rear units supplied the suspension, and long travel competition forks soaked up the bumps up front.

The development of this machine was equally interesting, and illustrated perfectly the success of Italjet. The new model sported cantilever suspension for the machine, something Italjet had considered themselves but rejected on the grounds of lack of space on the 145lb

Above: Leo Tartartini poses with the 50cc Italjet 1978 prototype scrambler. It uses the world's smallest cantilever type frame

Below: the 1973 Italjet Kangaroo used a 125cc engine developing 15bhp

Below: the unusual Italjet Pak-a-Way was launched at the London Motor Cycle Show in 1977 and featured a 50cc Morini engine. It was designed to fold up for convenience and used an automatic gearbox and an all-enclosed chain final drive system

machine with its fourteen-inch rear wheel. The British concessionaires, AGNI Ltd of Wallington in Surrey, decided otherwise and went ahead with their own development project. In 1976 they were satisfied they had perfected the system and sold the prototype to schoolboy scrambler Phillip Cranford, who went on to win 98 per cent or the 70 or so races he entered on it! By the middle of 1977 he was leading the Horsham and Portsmouth championships and was lying third in the national British Schoolboy Motocross Association Championships.

The modification was adopted by Italjet in all new models of the CX80R. Martin Hardiman, Managing Director of AGNI, enjoyed a very close relationship with the factory in Italy, as he did with all other concessionaires around the world. Between them all was a continual cross-changing of modifications, marketing information, spares distribution, and technical advice that exceeds by far any other motor cycle factories' operation.

Next on the list was a milder mannered bike, the CX100, intended to provide an ideal beginner's machine for the late starter in schoolboy scrambling. Its power output was mild, the bike was equipped with four gears, and was of the same dimensions as the CX80R. Engine was by Franco Morini. Both the CX80R and the CX100 were intended primarily, at least in Britain, for use in the eleven to thirteen-year-old Intermediate class of schoolboy scrambling.

Top of the scramblers was the new 125, a full blooded motocrosser in complete adult competition trim. In Britain this was used in the thirteen to sixteen-year-old Senior class of schoolboy scrambling, although on the Continent, where the 125 class was popular, in open grand prix events it proved to be immensely successful. Like the CX80R and the CX50R, it was a limited edition machine, built in small quantities, so demand always exceeded supply. In this case the engine was

built by Hiro, a little known Italian company introduced by Martin Hardiman to Leo Tartarini at the Milan show in 1975, when he saw the potential offered by the engine's use of reed valve induction and six gears.

Other motor cycles were produced, such as the 50cc road racer, although this was specifically intended to satisfy club racers within Italy. There was the Coyote 125, a smart 19bhp trial/enduro for both Italian and American markets where such machines were enjoying extreme popularity. There was, too, the Buccaneer, a 250 twin equipped with a Yamaha engine. Unfortunately it appeared, despite a huge demand, that it would not be seen in Britain. Its Italjet modification of electronic ignition apparently improved its power output over standard, and its handling and styling were reported to be considerably in advance of Yamaha's own similar 250.

Even so, the company made its money selling childrens' machinery. Where others played at it, they made a business of it, which is principally why they so utterly dominated all classes of schoolboy scrambling. Italjet were probably unique in motor cycling history in that respect.

DM

Above left: Italjet's Mini Bambino M5B model was fitted with 10-inch wheels and a 50cc motor

Above right: a 1977 Italjet Junior Cross Super Competition CX50S; it had a 50cc four-speed engine

Below: the 1977 Italjet Junior Cross Automatic JC5B; it also had a 50cc engine, but had an automatic gearbox

Italjet CX80R

When a customer pays nearly £500 for an 80cc machine, logic suggests that the bike must be something special, especially when the bike is destined for use by a nine-year-old child.

Italjet's little CX80R scrambler certainly is something special, although whether it is worth the money must be left to the purchaser to decide.

The CX80R, which stands only 41 inches high, is powered by a 79.6cc, air-cooled, single-cylinder Minarelli engine which develops a quite incredible 13bhp at 10,500rpm – enough power to bring the colour back to any self-respecting young pre-teenager's cheeks. The engine, incidentally, is fitted with Dansi magneto ignition and a VHB 22-BS Dellorto carburettor.

The CX80R is a perfect competition scrambles machine in miniature. It is also a very highly competitive machine for schoolboy scrambling. The reason for this is that the CX80R is a handbuilt bike. Production of the CX80R is very limited and each machine is hand built from selected parts in Italjet's competition shop. At present only eight units a day are manufactured.

The CX80R is fitted with a duplex frame and, like its grown-up Grand Prix counterparts, has long-travel, hydraulic front forks and gas-filled Marzocchi dampers at the rear.

In addition to its sturdy frame and powerful engine, the CX80R is fitted with a six-speed gearbox.

Knobbly tyres are used front and rear, 2.75 × 17s at the front and 3.50 × 14s at the rear.

Overall length of the little machine is 69 inches, wheelbase is 48 inches, height is 48 inches and overall width is 32 inches. Because of its small size and the lightweight materials used, the CX80R weighs in at 145lb.

The CX80R is suitable for youngsters of between nine and fifteen years of age and there can be no doubt that it is one of the most popular and competitive machines in action in schoolboy scrambling today.

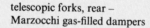

Engine
Air-cooled, single-cylinder two-stroke. 48mm (1.9in) bore × 44mm (1.7in) stroke = 79.6cc. Maximum power; 13bhp at 10,500rpm. Compression ratio 13.0:1. Kick-start on right-hand side

Transmission
Multiplate clutch in oil bath. Six-speed gearbox with left-hand side gearchange. Chain drive to rear wheel

Suspension
Front – hydraulic Paioli

telescopic forks, rear – Marzocchi gas-filled dampers

Brakes
Drums front and rear

Wheels and Tyres
2.75 × 17in front, 3.50in × 14in

rear

Weight
145lb (66kg)

Seating
Single seater for motocross racing use

Amid all the sound and fury of battle – the crump of exploding shells, the stuttering machine-guns, the swish of rockets – that characterised what has been described as The Longest Day, there came to many a British soldier struggling to establish a foothold on a Normandy beach, a homely and familiar note, the buzz of a lightweight two-stroke.

It could have been a little Royal Enfield. Equally, it could have been a 125cc Model ML James, of which nearly 300 were in action on the Normandy beaches during D-Day and thereafter. Some had been ferried across in landing craft, others had travelled with the airborne troops in their invasion gliders. Now, they were under the control of the beachmasters, scuttling across patches where heavier machines might have foundered, fetching and carrying, indi-cating the paths blasted through the enemy defences, and generally serving as mechanised sheepdogs.

The Model ML (the initials meant 'Military Lightweight') was by no means the James concern's only contribution to the war effort. With the introduction by Villiers in 1938 of the 98cc Junior auto-cycle engine, James had brought out their own version of a powered bicycle; it was well timed, for with the drastic fuel rationing of World War II, such an economical device was to prove invalu-able to those who could prove their need for independent transport. Between 1939 and 1945, almost 6000 machines were turned out, for the benefit of munitions shift workers, nurses and midwives, and others who had of necessity to be out and about at times when public transport was not available.

That was only part of the James war effort. Their works at Gough Road, Greet, was separated by a patch of open ground from the giant BSA plant and, like their BSA neighbours, James suffered considerable damage during the 1940 raids on Birmingham, but the scars were patched up, and shell cases, aircraft components, and similar war material continued to pour out of the factory.

Incidentally, a dozen or so rival makers were producing powered cycles (we would call them mopeds today) but, as yet, nobody had come up with a univers-ally accepted name for the type. All employed the 98cc Villiers Junior or, later, Junior De Luxe unit; but from the proliferation of Autobyks, Autoettes, Power Cycles, Powerbikes and suchlike, it was the James contribution – Autocycle – which caught on and became general.

It was in 1880 that Harry James, works manager of a Birmingham engineering company, took the bold decision to start out on his own as a maker of ordinary (that is, penny-farthing) bicycles. This was a bold decision indeed, for Harry was no youngster. However, he acquired a shop-cum-office in Constitution Hill, with workshop at the rear, and there he began the James Cycle Company, which title was to remain unaltered to the very end, 90 years later.

Trade flourished, larger premises became necessary, and 1890 saw Harry James installed in a bigger factory in Sampson Road North, Sparkbrook. Moreover, he could now afford to off-load some of the burden of running the company on to the shoulders of a manager, Charles Hyde.

However, Harry's connection with the firm which bore his name had now not much longer to run. In 1897 the James Cycle Company went public, and Mr James took the opportunity of retiring, leaving Charles Hyde in control. Unhappily, Harry survived to enjoy his retirement for only a few years more.

Thus far, production had been of pedal cycles entirely, but by the turn of the century several bicycle factories were toying with the idea of adding power to pedals. In 1902, Hyde took on an assistant. He was Fred Kimberley, a Coventry man who had been apprenticed to the Premier company and who had then gained some experience of early motor cycles at Hotchkiss, Mayo and Meek, whose Coventry-Eagle machines of the period used locally-produced MMC engines copied from De Dion.

Fred soon persuaded Charles Hyde that James, too, needed a motor cycle in the range, and the outcome was a typical machine of the day, with a Minerva engine clipped to the front-down tube of a strengthened bicycle frame, driving direct to a pulley on the rear wheel by a twisted rawhide belt. The price was £55.

There was, too, an alternative model at the same price. This one carried its engine within the frame diamond and, by means of a short chain, drove a friction roller pressed against the rear tyre. It would seem, though, that the friction-roller version was not too successful, because the only machine shown in the 1903 catalogue is the Model T, the one with the clip-on 2½hp Minerva engine.

By this time the Werner Brothers, over in Paris, had discovered the most logical position for the engine – at the base of the frame diamond, where a cycle's pedalling gear was usually housed. However, the scheme was patented, and the James company had to find a way round by building a loop frame in which to house the power unit – which, for 1904, was a Belgian-made FN.

All this was fairly orthodox, but there happened to be, in the Birmingham area, a very astute inventor named P.L. Renouf. It had been he who, in association with Accles and Turrell, had vastly improved the De Dion powered tricycle design by moving the engine from De Dion's original position, at the rear of the axle, to within the wheelbase. This, of course, made the machine much more stable. The idea was taken up by Ariel and Swift.

To the James company, Renouf proposed a highly unconventional motor cycle in which the wheels were carried on stub axles. There were hub-centre steering, and a fuel and oil tank carried in front of the steering column. For riding comfort, the saddle was mounted on two long flat springs.

Understandably, the new machine was the sensation of the November 1908 Stanley Show. For the first time, the engine (86 × 90mm) was of the James' firm's own design and construction, and featured concentric inlet and exhaust valves. The rear axle was 'live', with the wheel on one side of the frame bearing and the belt-drive pulley on the other. Dogs on the axle permitted the machine to be started, on its centre stand, by means of a crank handle.

The procedure for getting under way was for the rider to withdraw the outer flange of the engine-shaft pulley, so leaving the engine running but no longer driving the belt. He then raised the centre stand and climbed aboard; by operating a pedal, the engine-pulley flange could then be closed. This served as a friction take-up, and the machine moved off.

By this time, Fred Kimberley was Managing Director, as, indeed, he was to be for fifty years. The General Manager was Selby Arter whose father, John Arter, had been the firm's accountant back in Harry James's day.

As with all too many an advanced design, the public marvelled but did not buy, even though *Motor Cycle*, in its show report, commented: 'Mr Arter, the manager, assures us that he has driven it seven or eight hundred miles with perfect satisfaction.'

The one-sided James could make other claims to fame. It was almost certainly the first motor cycle to be equipped with

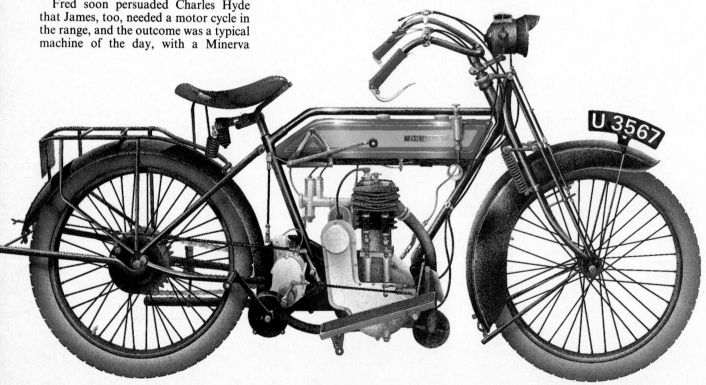

Left: a James sidecar outfit of 1914; it was one of the first motor cycles produced purely for the commercial market and featured such selling points as drive chain, two-speed gearbox and multiplate clutch

Below: a vee-twin 500cc sidevalve James of 1928

Bottom: the first consignment of James motor cycles produced following the end of World War II. The bikes were civilian versions of the ML125 model

Opposite page: a 4½hp single-cylinder James of 1913

internal expanding brakes (whereby bronze shoes operated in a steel drum). And it introduced the staggered 'pine-apple' arrangement of cylinder fins that was to be seen on James-built engines for a number of years to come.

During the next couple of years, the 'safety' James underwent steady development. In its final form, for the 1911 season, it had an orthodox side-valve engine, conventional seat mounting, and a form of parallel-ruler front fork springing. The front tank was now for oil only, and a separate saddle tank contained petrol. The original type of belt drive, with the engine pulley serving as clutch, was still available, but at extra cost there was the more sophisticated alternative of a metal-to-metal clutch in the rear hub.

There would seem to be no logical reason why a machine with wheels mounted on one side only should not succeed. Scooters with such an arrangement were to be accepted quite readily in the years to come, but in 1911 the public

just wasn't ready for such a radical departure, and even the James people were losing faith, because flanking the 'safety' model at that year's London Show (by this time staged at Olympia) was a motor cycle of more orthodox appearance but which, nevertheless, was of extremely advanced conception. Its most noticeable feature was a two-speed countershaft gearbox incorporating a multi-plate clutch with alternate steel and bronze plates. Transmission was all-chain, with the primary chain housed in a cast-light-alloy casing, and the rear chain in a casing with detachable end to allow the rear wheel to be extracted.

That all-metal clutch was to remain a James feature right into the 1930s. It was, too, to find special favour among speed-

THE FIRST
CONSIGNMENT
OF
JAMES
MOTOR CYCLES

1955
JAMES 150 c.c. Cadet
Model J.15

way riders in due course and one, at least, was still being employed in league racing as late as the 1960s.

Indeed, 1911 was quite a notable year for James in many ways. In addition to the introduction of the new designs they had acquired a subsidiary in the Osborn company, of Tower Works, Newtown Row; this had been started by Fred J. Osborn, a famous racing cyclist, and was one of the earliest cycle firms to produce a lightweight two-stroke motor cycle. Renamed Osmonds (1911) Ltd, and transferred to the premises that had been erected three years previously at Greet, this was to provide a useful second-string label in later years.

By 1913, James had a two-stroke of their own, with the characteristic 'pine-apple' fin arrangement and a smart finish of two-tone brown. It partnered the 600cc 'big single', the engine of which had been made more compact by mounting the magneto behind the cylinder. Already on the stocks was yet another model, and this one was to be the firm favourite of many a rider in the next few decades.

Introduced in 1914, this was the 500cc Model 7 side-valve twin, with three-speed gearbox and, again, enclosed all-chain drive. However, war clouds were looming on the horizon, and soon production of the twin had to be dropped, so that Greet could concentrate on ammunition. The company was not asked to build machines for the British Army, but some twins were supplied to the allies for wartime use.

With the return of peace, the James came back to the market, but, before the company was fully back in its stride, the works were badly damaged by fire, and full production was not resumed until 1922. The first really new model was a 7hp twin, specifically for sidecar work, with interchangeable wheels. Under the Osmond name, there was a neat autocycle with the engine, like that of the P & M, taking the place of the front-down tube.

Through the 1920s, James prospered, offering the public a wide range of machines—two-strokes, side-valves, over-head-valves, singles and vee-twins. By 1928, there was an overhead-valve version of the 500cc twin, and like many another manufacturer, James caught the speedway bug. Their offering was a stripped and strutted version of the twin, and though its performance on the track was spectacular rather than speedy, it was adored by spectators mainly because, in the words of *Motor Cycle* speedway columnist, it was 'so sonorously vocal!'. The speedway twin was not a total flop, and in later years one example was to do quite a spot of cleaning-up at grass-tracks in the North London area.

For a while, James abandoned manufacture of their own two-stroke engines and, instead, employed Villiers units of 150, 172 and 196cc, but there was a return in 1932 with a James engined one-fifty. Meanwhile, the enterprising little Baker Motor Cycles company had been acquired, and this brought to the James programme the 'Baker Patent Brazeless

Frame'. Like Francis-Barnett, Frank Baker (who, earlier, had founded and operated the Precision works) had devised a frame employing straight tubes and a bolted-up construction. For a year or two, James continued to build bikes with the Baker name on the tank, but then replaced these by James models built under Baker patents. Frank Baker, himself, joined the sales staff of James.

Gradually, the manufacture of engines was dropped, and a lightweights-only policy took its place, with machines from 98 to 250cc, all employing Villiers units. The last engine to be built at Greet was something of an anachronism, for it was a 750cc vee-twin side valve with one-piece cylinder barrel and head; this was the power unit of the James Samson Handy-van, a commercial three-wheeler made until the mid 1930s, with a payload of 5cwt.

The return to peacetime production in 1946 saw James with a two-model range, comprising the Autocycle, and the Model ML 125cc, the latter out of Army service khaki and dressed in maroon and grey. Sport was just beginning to get under way again, and the James factory joined in with a trials team – all on Model ML one-two-fives at first – known far and wide as 'Three Normans'; they were Norman Hooton, Norman Moore, and Norman Palmer, and their exploits gained James much valuable publicity.

Naturally, the two-port Model ML was but an interim measure, and with the expansion of the Villiers engine range

JAMES *Cavalier 175*

came a wider choice of James roadsters and competition mounts. One of the best-known of these later Villiers engines was the unit-construction 197cc Mark 8E, with the aid of which a very competitive little trials model was devised.

In 1951, James was taken into the Associated Motor Cycles group, and in due course a range of machines employing 150, 175, 199 and 250cc engines made in the Woolwich factory of the parent AMC concern, was marketed. These were notable for the considerable use of pressed steel in the frame construction of such models as the Cadet, Cavalier and Commodore.

James joined the scooter movement, too, with a rather heavy-looking 150cc model in which the engine lay under the floor section, cylinder pointing forward. In fact this was a clever idea, because it gave a better weight distribution than was possible when, as in imported machines, the engine was mounted within the rear bodywork.

In the James, the whole of the under-seat area could be used for parcel carrying. The frame, too, was ingenious, with its main members so widely spaced that they outlined the apron and floor, and, in consequence, served to protect machine and rider from the possible effects of an accident.

Several years before, Donald S. Heather of the parent AMC group had declared that scooters were only a passing craze. Eventually, even he had to admit that they had their advantages, but by the time James started work on their own machine it was already too late. Imported scooters such as the Lambretta and Vespa had gained too big a hold on the British market; with all their superior resources, not even BSA could make any impression and, anyway, in the eyes of scooter riders accustomed to the daintiness of Italian styling, the James was just too clumsy-looking. It achieved only minimal sales, and failed to recoup the company's outlay on bodywork press tools.

Under Norman Moore, the competitions department continued to thrive, and in the days immediately before the coming of the Bultaco, the Cotswold trials model – as demonstrated by riders such as Garth Wheldon – achieved a fair measure of popularity. The Cotswold had its scrambles counterpart in the Commando, and here Chris Horsfield was engaged to keep the James banner flying. (A decade earlier, there had even been some road-racing successes by a 197cc James which was prepared and ridden by Bill Lomas, but that was strictly a private venture.)

The factory bread-and-butter model was still the Cadet, now with 150cc AMC engine and a tubular-and-pressed-steel composite frame, and with an undamped coil spring to provide a measure of rear-end comfort. Higher up the capacity scale, the 199cc Captain retained a considerable following, and a mildly hotted-up version, the Sports Captain, was the preferred choice of youngsters who wanted to cut a dash with the girls. Topping the range was the remarkably handsome Superswift, which utilised the 250cc Villiers 4T twin.

Although they concentrated on the smaller-capacity end of the market, James were especially vulnerable to the new generation of lightweights which, as the 1960s advanced, began to flood in from Japan.

In an attempt to come to terms with the invaders, AMC formed a working partnership under the title of Suzuki (GB) Ltd. They even (thereby adding insult to injury) hived off a part of the James works, to serve as office, warehouse, and service department for Suzuki. Still, the Suzuki people did have the decency to use the back entrance to the plant, quoting Golden Hillock Road, instead of Gough Road, as the address.

Yet time was running out fast for James. The last new machine to carry the honoured name on its tank panels was another version of the utility 150cc Cadet, this time with the engine suspended from a large-diameter-tube backbone frame. It was an interesting design, but it only made little impact because AMC were now deep in the financial mire. In the ensuing crash, James disappeared. The factory was sold to a pump manufacturer, and, after a short while, even the outline of the James shield, which had graced the iron gates of the office entrance, had vanished. FG

Opposite page: the 150cc James Cadet Model J15 of 1955

Above: the 1959 James Cavalier 175 (left) and the James Commodore model of 1950, pictured on the right

Below left: the attractive James Sports Captain of 1964 had a 199cc engine

Below right: many of the James models were designed for the commuter market; this is the 122cc Cadet De Luxe of 1951

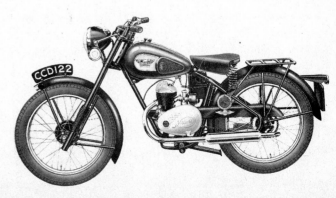

A Pole Apart

But for serious injuries Edward Jancarz could have been Poland's first world speedway champion. Instead that honour fell to rank outsider Jerzy Szczakiel who beat Ivan Mauger in Poland in 1973 in a run-off in which the famous New Zealander crashed.

When just 22, Jancarz made his world final debut in 1968 at Ullevi Stadium, Sweden, a complete unknown. Fourteen races later Eddie Jancarz was third in the world, standing alongside world champion Ivan Mauger and runner-up Barry Briggs, on the winners' rostrum. He had tied on points with that year's Continental champion Gennady Kurilenko from Russia and beaten him for the third place. The speedway hungry Poles had obviously come up with a star, even though he had had to fight injury to get to that first World Final. In a crash in which Norwegian Sverre Harrfeldt was seriously hurt in the European final in Wroclaw, Poland, Jancarz broke some ribs, but still rode later to make the cut to the final.

If he could grab third in his first World Final, the championship could be his. In 1969 he made the final again, which was held at Wembley, never a happy

hunting ground for Iron Curtain riders. The young Jancarz snatched only three points from his first three rides and had crashed with Swedish ace Torbjorn Harryson, who had broken a leg, but Jancarz came back and won his last two rides to give him nine points and a sixth in the world placing.

However, in the next couple of seasons, 1970 and 1971 when he should have consolidated his world championship form, he was the victim of injuries, including a troublesome collar bone problem which bugged him time and time again.

Dark, swarthy-skinned Jancarz, with his mop of Beatle style hair, never was a typical Polish rider. The Poles always had a reputation for throttle bashing, which suited wide open, big speed circuits, but which soon got them into trouble on the smaller, tighter European tracks.

Jancarz, on the other hand, always was a superb speedway stylist and a master of the fine art of throttle control, as he displayed many times on tour in England, Australia and New Zealand. He commanded great respect amongst the top riders, for they all know when Jancarz got it altogether, he could beat

anybody, anywhere. This respect was shown when he was invited to join the famous Ivan Mauger/Barry Briggs world champions troupe series in 1974 and 1976.

If he had ridden, 1970 could have been Jancarz's year. The World Final had been allocated behind the Iron Curtain for the first time. In the huge Wroclaw stadium, Polish riders Pawel Waloszek, Antoni Woryna and Henryk Glucklich were second, third and fourth, but none of them could stop Ivan Mauger clinching his third world title in a row. No one will ever know if Jancarz could have gone one better than his fellow countrymen. In 1971, Jancarz was only part fit for most of the season and was not allowed to enter the world championship by his Polish federation.

In 1972 he re-emerged from the international shadows to reach the Continental final of the world championships, but scored only two points. In 1973, 1974, 1975 and 1976 Jancarz booked a World Final place but never found the form that took him to his third place overall in 1968. In 1973 he was eleventh with six points, in 1974 he scored one point from a reserve berth, in 1975 he scored four points and in 1976, five points.

Jancarz's lack of latter day success has been mirrored by the rest of the Polish riders too. At one stage Poland looked likely to be the number one speedway nation, with successes in the

hardest of all team competitions, the World Team Cup. But they were always up and down and failed to stay the course. Their one moment of real glory was in 1973 when, right out of the blue, they had their first ever world champion in Jerzy Szczakiel, but he never again repeated anything like that title winning form.

It still could be Jancarz who will guide his country's fortunes for it was rumoured that 1977 was to be his last riding year and he would take up the appointment of national coach in 1978. Representations were made by the British Speedway Promoters Association to the Poles before the start of the 1977 British season for them to send half a dozen of their top stars to join British League clubs for the year. In the end only two did so. Jancarz joined the famous Wimbledon Dons at plush Plough Lane, while one of the new wave of Poles, Marek Cieslak joined fellow Londoners, White City.

Jancarz had a hard job to do. Wimbledon were without a number one following the tragic death of their top star Tommy Jansson in 1976, but the crowd quickly took the likeable Pole to their hearts, especially after he won his first-ever race for them in Dons colours. The Poles had for years been trying to 'westernise' their speedway because they knew that was the only way to become a world power. They had tried to cut down the size of their huge tracks, so that their riders could master these and so master British style tracks too. Undoubtedly Jancarz stored up a wealth of information from his year-long stay on the way British speedway was handled. AE

Opposite page, far left: Ed Jancarz wearing the body colours of his British team, the Wimbledon 'Dons'

Opposite page, near left: Jancarz, almost unrecognisable under his face mask and goggles

Above: Jancarz is one of the most stylish riders ever to come out of Poland and quickly adapted to the shorter and tighter British tracks. Here he slips inside England and Reading ace John Davies at a meeting during 1977

Left: Edward Jancarz riding for the Rest of the World team against England during an International meeting in 1977

Success was Pencilled in

Once upon a time, just around the turn of the present century, the infant British motor cycle industry was almost wholly reliant on engines imported from France, Germany, or Belgium. As an alternative there was the Coventry-made MMC, but even that was merely a De Dion built under licence.

Then along came one John Alfred Prestwich, to design and manufacture the first truly successful all-British proprietary engine, and from that moment on any potential motor cycle tycoon had no further need to shop abroad. By the time the JAP engine reached its fiftieth birthday, in 1953, well over a million units had been despatched – and not only to British bike factories, because quite a substantial number were employed by German, Italian, Swedish and other overseas motor cycle makers (research, however, has failed to turn up a Jap-JAP!).

Some engines drove humdrum little ride-to-work models, while others lived beneath fuel tanks on which were inscribed such glamour names as Zenith, Coventry-Eagle Flying-8, or, most glamorous of all, Brough Superior. JAP-engined machines won road races by the many hundred, captured world speed records in just about every capacity class on two wheels and three, and totally dominated the speedway world for something like 40 years.

Born in Kensington in 1874, John Prestwich was a natural engineer. He built a working model of a stationary steam engine at the age of 14 and, two years later, already held patents in respect of combustion engine improvements.

At 20 years of age, he was the chief of the J.A. Prestwich Manufacturing Company, which sounded most impressive but which was actually himself, with one lathe and a set of hand tools, operating in his father's greenhouse. Still, that was just temporary accommodation, and in 1895 he opened a small works in Tottenham, North London.

At that time his principal interest lay in making scientific instruments and electrical apparatus, and it was because of this that he became involved with William Friese-Greene, the inventor of cinematography. No fewer than 16 of Prestwich's experiments in this field are currently housed in the Science Museum, South Kensington. One JAP camera travelled with Scott to the Antarctic. Another filmed Queen Victoria's Diamond Jubilee procession through London in 1898.

Prestwich turned his attention to designing a motor cycle engine in 1901, but it was to be another two years before the

Above: from scientific instrument and camera manufacture, JAP graduated to building motor cycles in 1903. This is one of the first models of that year, with a 293cc, 2¼bhp engine

Below: JAP built their first vee-twin as early as 1903 with competition use very much in mind. This is a racing engine of 1930, one of a JAP range for that year which encompassed over forty models

first JAP was put into production. It was of 293cc (70 × 76mm bore and stroke) producing 2¼bhp at 1600rpm, and a contemporary description in *Motor Cycle* remarked on the especially notable cleanness and regularity of the castings.

In the manner of the day, the new JAP employed an automatic (suction operated) inlet valve. The crankcase embodied a JAP-patented vacuum valve 'to prevent the ejectment of oil' (presumably this was a type of crankcase breather). Lubrication was by a constant drip actuated by the suction of the piston.

Not only was the new engine offered to existing motor cycle manufacturers like Triumph (which had begun operations, the previous year, with an imported Minerva engine) but JAP themselves went into business as bike builders, in opposition to their own engine customers. A works-entered JAP took part in the Auto-Cycle Club's 1000-mile Trial of 1903. Another, with a 90-degree vee-twin engine and ridden by Charles B. Franklin – who, years later, became designer and vice-president of Indian – represented England in the early International Cup Races. Not until 1908 did JAP concentrate on engines alone.

A single-cylinder JAP engine powered the Matchless with which Charlie Collier won the first-ever Isle of Man TT. An 8hp overhead-valve twin gave Harry Bashall (BAT) victory in the first Brooklands 1000cc race, in 1909.

It was in 1909, also, that Will Cook of the North London Garage company arrived at the Brooklands track with a vast 1400cc overhead-valve NLG-JAP twin. His intention was to attack the world flying-mile and flying-kilometer records standing to the credit of Henri Cissac's big Peugeot, but although he didn't quite hit that target, at least Cook set up a new Brooklands track record.

In fact, the JAP works had built three of the 1400cc monster engines. Another went to Harry Bashall, but there is no record of him having used it. The third went to Harry Collier, who first built it into a Matchless frame; finding the machine unmanageable, he extracted the engine and, instead, fitted it to an experimental Matchless monoplane. Sad to say, the 'plane crashed on take-off from Woolwich Arsenal playing fields.

That wasn't the first JAP-powered 'plane, though. Prestwich had built a successful one himself, and another JAP engine was employed by Alliott Verdon-Roe in the first Avro monoplane, successfully flight-tested on Clapton marshes.

In the run-up to World War I, JAP were faced with competition from other British engine firms including TDC and Precision yet managed to stay triumphantly on top. The works at Lansdowne Road, Tottenham were expanded, and expanded again, but one addition to the factory was for a rather unexpected purpose.

It came about because James Alfred Prestwich had been posed a technical problem, how to produce and paint lead pencils efficiently. He came up with the answer in due course, but by that time the enquirer had gone out of business; so rather than waste all the research that had been expended, JAP went into pencil manufacture themselves, setting up the subsidiary company of Pencils Ltd to make pencils at ten times the rate that had been possible earlier.

The motor cycling boom of the early 1920s saw many new small companies start up, and JAP found themselves working at full stretch on a programme extending from 150cc two-strokes to big ohv and sv vee-twins. They were no longer motor cycle builders in their own right, but it was necessary to keep abreast of technological development. Consequently JAP-entered machines made regular appearances at Brooklands (on three wheels as well as two, because JAP development engineer E.B. Ware was a well-known competitor on Morgan three-wheelers).

Below: since the end of World War II, JAP's major involvement with motor cycle engines – as opposed to industrial engines – has been in speedway racing. This is a cutaway of a 1968 497cc engine for the sport. The motor used an Elektron crankcase, a steel or duralumin con-rod and a cast iron cylinder head. It breathed through an Amal Concentric carburettor

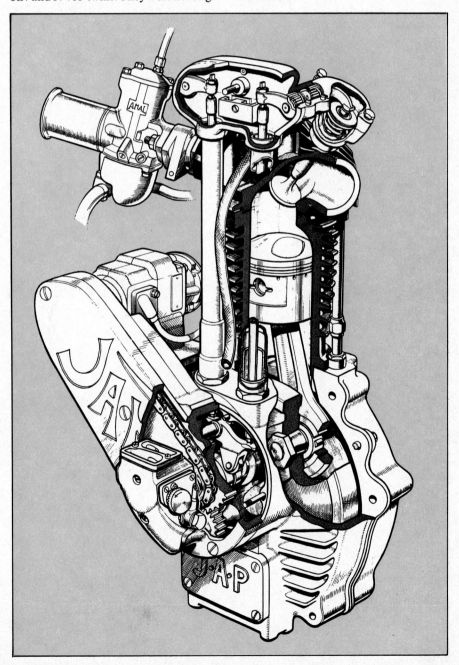

Design responsibility was largely that of Stanley Greening, but in the earlier 1920s a brilliant young designer was a member of the JAP staff. He was Valentine Page, who in due course was to go on to do wonders at Ariel, BSA and Triumph. Val Page's masterpiece for JAP was an extremely advanced five-stud, double-overhead-camshaft 350cc engine numbered EXP1. Mounted in a New Imperial frame, this engine was used by Bert Le Vack in the 1922 Junior TT. Bert set up a new lap record, and led the race for three laps until forced out by gearbox troubles. At Brooklands, it narrowly missed being the first 350cc to lap at 100mph. Later, fitted with a smaller-bore cylinder, it brought Le Vack a hatful of 250cc-class records at over 80mph. Certainly the overhead-camshaft engine was potent, but it was too complicated to produce economically as a catalogued job, and it was shelved in favour of a pushrod ohv model.

In 1923, JAP patented a desmodromic-gear layout, whereby both valves were opened and closed positively by a mechanism which looked much akin to that of a railway locomotive. It was not proceeded with, probably because of the pressure of work on the standard engines. Indeed, the JAP programme of the 1920s included 28 different models – or, if all the available options were taken into account, something like double that number.

Said *Motor Cycling*, of the 1928 range: 'Eventually the special racing engine becomes the standard racing engine, which in due course becomes the sports pattern, while what is perhaps this year's sports engine is next year the touring. For instance, the 1925 Senior TT was won on a machine fitted with what is now the 500cc sports engine.'

Below: JAP engines found their way onto three wheels as well as onto two: this is a water-cooled vee-twin with magneto ignition, as used on a 1927 Morgan Aero

Nevertheless, most manufacturers had the ultimate aim of building motor cycles powered by engines of their own design and make, and use of a JAP was but a means to this end. New Imperial, one of JAP's major customers, switched over completely by the later 1920s; Matchless, big JAP users at one time, had long since left the fold and even OK Supreme, while still using JAP power for everyday models, were eventually to employ their own overhead-camshaft engines for the classier end of their range.

It was an unhappy 1934 Senior TT experience with JAP engines that determined Phil Vincent to have done with proprietary units, and go in for designing and building his own. Soon, Cotton and AJW were virtually the only British-based customers left.

Yet in one field the JAP reigned unchallenged. As far back as 1930, Stan Greening and speedway ace Wal Phillips had concocted the first speedway unit, largely by adapting a road-racing engine, and it was so fantastically successful that it was to rule the dirt-tracks of Britain, Australia and the USA right through to the coming of the Jawa in the 1960s.

Incidentally, in the years from 1920 to 1939, the JAP company prefixed the engine numbers with an apparent jumble of letters which, however, indicated size, and type. More importantly, the letter following the oblique mark (for instance 'KTC/N') was the key to the date of manufacture. For the ten-year span from 1920 to 1929, the JAP code-word was PNEUMATICS, where P indicated 1920, N was 1921, and so on up to S for 1929. Between 1930 and 1939 another ten-letter code was necessary, in which none of the letters had occurred earlier. There was no such word, and so the company settled for the gibberish WHYZDRVFOG.

As the motor cycle side declined, so JAP production leant more and more on the industrial engine business. Thousands of Model 2A stationary units were supplied for such purposes as battery charging during World War II. With the end of the war, JAP announced new engines – a vertical-twin side valve, 125cc two-stroke, 250cc overhead-camshaft twin (never produced), and a range of racing engines including a 1000cc vee-twin for Cooper cars.

The impact of JAP on the post-war motor cycle world was minimal, and by the time the company merged with Villiers in 1957, production was almost entirely of industrial engines. In 1977, the JAP name still lived on in the speedway engine, hand-built to special order by George Greenwood, who had acquired the manufacturing rights; although overshadowed by the Weslake and Jawa, it still had a faithful circle of followers, and in the four-valve version being offered by Neil Street, was set for a come-back. FG

Circuit in the sun

First used for a world championship motor cycle race in 1969, the Jarama circuit near Madrid has failed to match its rival Montjuich Park, Barcelona, in atmosphere, spectator appeal or popularity with competitors.

The Spanish Federation had thought of using the circuit in 1968 to stage the Spanish GP, but the best the Madrid circuit could hope to attract was a crowd of about 20,000, so financial considerations ruled the day and Barcelona was given the plum meeting.

When the big day at Jarama arrived in 1969 most people were disappointed that the change had been made! The 2.2 mile circuit, with its twists and turns, failed to produce exciting racing, and torrential rain showers and strong winds kept the crowd down to a low level.

Even worse was the organisation problems before and during the meeting. The riders, many not in the best of tempers after long arguments with Spanish customs officers at the border, then found themselves forced to use a very poor quality fuel for practice. Though high octane the petrol wouldn't mix with the vegetable based oil used by the two stroke brigade.

After Rod Gould had presented the organisers with a petition, they agreed to supply a lower octane fuel that did mix with the oil, but for many competitors practice had been a frustrating and unproductive occasion.

The racing was dramatic, though, with Italian Giacomo Agostini overcoming tumbles in both practice and races to win both the 350cc and 500cc events. In the big race Ago was chasing fellow countryman Angelo Bergamonti on the Paton twin, and Australian Kel Carruthers riding the 382cc Aermacchi single, when Kel slid off, and in the confusion Ago was brought down, too.

He was helped to his feet by Carruthers, and set off in pursuit of Bergamonti. Within seven laps he had pulled back the half lap lead, and Giacomo went on to win. Earlier he won the 350cc event, using his spare MV after the best one had been damaged in a crash during practice.

Spanish hero Santiago Herrero won the 250cc race to keep the locals happy, and an unknown Spaniard, Salvador Caniellas, led the wet and soggy 125cc event for 17 of the 30 laps before being forced to retire on a prototype 125cc Yamaha production racer.

Everyone was glad to be back at Barcelona in 1970, but a year later the Spanish GP was once again staged at Jarama, and again the meeting was the centre of controversy. Arriving at the circuit there were no signs of a paddock, and apparently no entrance or exit gates either! But once in the paddock the problems were not over. Despite many letters and telegrams, riders had heard little or nothing from the organisers before the event, and many had to finalise their negotiations on practice day. To make matters worse the organisers only spoke Spanish!

Crowd control on race day provided some memorable, but unwanted, scenes. The fans spilled on to the track at the end of the 350cc event which opened the meeting, and the scenes were repeated, with even greater enthusiasm at the end of the 125cc race which Angel Nieto, the hard riding little Spaniard, won to clinch the world title. The men behind Nieto just had to stop, or crash into the fans. It was chaos, but at the end of the day the organisers revealed that they were in no position to run

Above: Britain's Chas Mortimer blasts off the line at Jarama in 1973 on his way to a superb victory in the 125cc Spanish Grand Prix. Mortimer was riding a Yamaha

Virage Ascari

Virages Portago

Virages de
Monza

Virages Farina

Rampa
Pegaso

Eses de
Bugatti

Virage Varzi

Virage Fangio

Virages de
la Mans

Virage Nuvolari

Virages del Tunel

the meeting, and the Spanish federation were unable to subsidize them. A petition was drawn up, and signed by the top liners of the day, requesting the FIM to stage future GPs at Barcelona, and never, ever return to Jarama. The FIM did little or nothing about the justified complaints, and to make matters even worse there were suggestions that some of the signatures on the list, including those of Chas Mortimer, Rod Gould, Phil Read, Jarno Saarinen and Jack Findlay, were forgeries!

Two years after that fiasco the Grand Prix, after being run the previous season at Barcelona, returned to Jarama. This time, although the crowd was still less than a quarter of those that normally line the picturesque Montjuich Park, the meeting passed off without any serious incidents.

The GP was back in Jarama in 1973, and it was the last time that the fans would see a 500cc championship race as part of the programme. Giacomo Agostini had long since clinched the world title, and, lured by the offer of a lot of money, he rode at an international meeting at the picturesque Cadwell Park circuit in England.

However, his team mate in the MV squad, Phil Read, needed points to ensure runner up spot in the 500cc class, and he won, but not without being chased by Swiss newcomer Bruno Kneubuhler on a Yamaha twin which had been enlarged to 351cc.

There was a surprise in the 350cc race, though, where young wealthy Brazilian Adu Celso Santos notched up his first ever GP win, beating the late Billie Nelson and Patrick Pons. Australian John Dodds won the 250cc event, with Kneubuhler second and Chas Mortimer third, and it was Mortimer who went on to create the biggest upset of the weekend. On his Yamaha he beat Angel Nieto in the 125cc race, leaving the Spanish fans speechless. Nieto was now on the works Morbidellis, but Chas Mortimer was in superb form on his Yamaha twin.

Without a GP to their credit in 1974, the Madrid-based organisers decided to run, instead, a round of the new FIM Formula 750 championship. The race clashed with an event at the Paul Ricard circuit in France leaving John Dodds a fairly easy win. He led the race from start to finish, and on the way to victory came within a tenth of the absolute lap record he had himself set the previous year. The twisty Jarama circuit was made to measure for the 350cc Yamaha twin, but Australian Jack Findlay did well to take his three-cylinder Suzuki into second spot, 27 seconds down on Dodds. A scrap for third place, between Spaniard Victor Palomo on 750 Ducati twin and Hans Muhlebach on a 350 Yamaha went in the local rider's favour.

The supporting races were dominated by Spanish stars. Benjamin Grau beat Dodds (Yamaha) in the 250cc class, leaving Angel Nieto on another factory Derbi well behind. Grau won the 125cc race, too, with Nieto, slowed by gear linkage trouble fourth.

Even that bonus, however, could not turn the meeting into anything other than a king size flop. The fans preferred watching bullfights, television or even Real Madrid football rather than take a twenty mile trip down the motorway from Madrid.

Without a 500cc race on the card the 350cc solo class topped the bill at the 1975 Spanish GP, and the race gave Italian Giacomo Agostini chance to inflict a defeat on the young Venezulan Johnny Cecotto, revenge for the tough treatment Johnny had handed out to Ago earlier in the year. Ago beat his young rival by almost ten seconds, but the pair were still close to a full minute ahead of third finisher, the Japanese rider Hideo Kanaya.

Hopes that Benjamin Grau, on the works Derbi, might win the 250cc race were dashed when Walter Villa rushed away into the distance, and Grau was beaten to the line by French youngster Patrick Pons, by three tenths of a second. Grau had been quickest in the 125cc class, too, but the factory machine broke, leaving Paolo Pileri on the works Morbidelli to win. Angel Nieto, now riding the rapid Van Veen Kreidler, won the 50cc class, so there was at least a small spot on consolation for the dispirited supporters.

With the Grand Prix at Barcelona, again, in 1976, the Jarama promoters elected to run a round of the FIM Formula 750 series. It was a disaster. The regulations were chopped and changed around in the weeks leading up to the event, and right up until the last moment it looked as though the race might be cancelled. Rather than make the long trip many of the leading contenders decided not to go, and those that did later had a great deal of respect for the stayaways because the meeting turned into a complete disaster.

Originally the race was to be a single event, over 90 kilometres. That would have been too short a distance to count in the title series, but a last minute change of plan increased the

---

Opposite page: Adu Celso Santos, winner of the 1973 350cc Spanish Grand Prix, in action at Jarama circuit (inset)

Below: Guido Marsovsky's Yamaha leads a group of machines at Jarama, a circuit which has a poor reputation among riders and is best known as a car racing track

programme to two 100 mile legs.

The advertising announced that stars like Giacomo Agostini, Steve Baker, Johnny Cecotto and Gary Nixon would be among the line-up, but it was a case of wishful thinking on the part of the promoters. In fact, the entry was so poor that several local competitors on a hotch-potch of machines were drafted in to the meeting! But if the entry was thin on the ground, the crowd, on both practice and race days, was so small it was possible to count the grandstand customers.

Half an hour before the first leg was due to start on Saturday evening a rain shower left the track wet and slippery. The riders asked the organisers to switch the race to Sunday morning, but they refused, and an hour later they finally dropped the flag. Visibility was now very poor, and there seemed a real danger that it would be dark before the full distance was completed. Frenchman Christian Estrosi took the lead from fellow countryman Michel Rougerie after just one lap, but with the race seemingly in his pocket he arrived at one corner which had been dry the previous lap, only to discover it was now wet. Down he went, and Rougerie went on to win from Victor Palomo. Only ten riders out of sixteen starters finished the race.

The second leg, on Sunday, started on time but it was a good thing that it did. Apparently the marshals had told the organisers that if there was a delay they would leave the circuit by 12.30pm as they all wanted to watch Real Madrid play football on television in the afternoon! Such are the problems of the organisers at Jarama.

Estrosi crashed again, and Rougerie took the lead, but after breaking the lap record he slowed, and Victor Palomo went on to win leaving Rougerie as the overall victor. Only six riders crossed the finishing line this time, but it was enough to let the results, such as they were, stand for the series.

This fiasco did not deter the organisers. In 1977 the Jarama circuit staged both a round of the new Formula 750cc world championship, and the Spanish GP. It was difficult to say which was the most boring, but probably the F750 meeting would win that contest, on points!

American Steve Baker seeking the world title for the Yamaha factory was obliged to go, and so were a handful on

Continentals still hopeful of pipping Steve to the crown, or at least taking runner up place in the championship. But the others, remembering the disasters of the past and, hardly overwhelmed at the miserable expenses offered, either stayed away or raced elsewhere.

As had happened the previous season, only 16 riders started in the race, run as a straight, 60 lap, 126 mile event on Sunday morning. The meeting failed to capture the imagination of the crowd, and fewer than 5000 fans made the trip. Steve Baker won the race, but he had a shock after his pit stop when surplus fuel made life difficult for him, and Dutchman Boet van Dulmen took the chance to go ahead. With just fifteen laps left, and holding a seven seconds lead, Boet crashed. Baker won, almost a minute up on French youngster Christian Sarron, and extended his lead in the series to fifteen points. Only nine men went the distance, and all collected championship points in a meeting that scarcely deserved such prestige.

The Grand Prix, a month later was much more attractive to the fans and more than double the number of spectators lined the circuit for the meeting. There were a few moments of drama in the meeting, and a few good individual performances too, but even record laps in the 50cc, 125cc and 250cc events could not drag the event from out of the realms of utterly boring mediocrity.

Angel Nieto won the 50cc race, despite a record breaking lap from Italian Eugenio Lazzarini on the Van Veen Kreidler, but Nieto on the works Bultaco was forced to stop early in the 125cc event. Takazumi Katayama won the 250cc race after Englishman Barry Ditchburn had crashed after running over a piece of perspex when leading the field on the Kawasaki. The 350cc race went to Frenchman Michel Rougerie, giving him his first ever win in this class, but like the rest of the programme there was little to get excited about.

Just how long it will be before financial pressures close down the man-made Jarama circuit is difficult to say. But the truth is that few would mourn its passing.   CJ

Below: since 1973, no 500cc Grand Prix has been held at Jarama. That year's event saw Phil Read score an impressive victory on the magnificent MV Agusta

Small guy standing out

Who was the rider who could tame the 50 horsepower Weslake speedway motor and be equally at home with the subtle power of a Bultaco trials bike? The answer is Reading maestro Dave Jessup.

Diminutive Jessup, he stood just five feet five inches in his socks, had always enjoyed trials riding. It was a means of keeping fit during the long winter months off from his regular trade of 'professional speedway rider' but he enjoyed winning trials as well.

Jessup was born in Suffolk and made his name through the Kent Youth Motor Cycle Club grass track events. He became club champion at 15, but he longed for his sixteenth birthday to come along. Then he was able to join the Eastbourne Eagles in the British League, Division Two. Although he was then the youngest rider in speedway he had a few rides for one of the most prestigious names in the sport, Division One's famous West Ham Hammers.

In 1970 he caught the eye of another famous London team, the revitalised Wembley Lions, who raced at the famous Cup Final stadium, but he still completed a full season for Eastbourne. As their number one for the year he qualified for the big Division Two meeting of the year, the Riders' Championship at Hackney's Waterden Road.

Jessup had to defy a Speedway Control Board ban to win the title, as the authorities thought, even at that tender age, he was too good to be entered and should be considered a full time First Division rider! After a day of argument the young flyer was allowed to compete – and won convincingly from Barry Crowson and the late Gary Peterson. He went to the tapes for his last race having scored four wins. Although outgated in his last ride he kept his cool, collected two points for second place and wrote his name in the speedway history books by becoming the youngest ever champion.

The teenage whiz kid became an established Young England cap with rides against the Czechs, Swedes and Australasia, also in 1970. He established himself as a favourite with the London crowds as a Wembley Lion before moving to another Lions den at Leicester in 1972. Here he became part of one of speedway's best one/two rider combinations of any team, with England captain Ray Wilson.

It was the same year that Jessup made his first impact in the world championship. He reached the British final, but failed to qualify for his first World Final, scoring only seven points, He had to wait until 1974 to reach the goal that all speedway riders seek, a World Final appearance: he had done it at the tender age of 21. The Wembley specialist had to go back to Wembley for the biggest night of his life for the European final. His goal of a World Final place seemed to slip, when in his first ride he had engine failure – and no points – but he stormed back with a win over the man who went on to take the European title, Peter Collins, and eight points in all saw him safely through to the final in Sweden.

He made a steady debut, scoring five points, on a very wet and heavy track.

Below: Dave Jessup stands only 5ft 5in tall but has won the hearts of speedway fans around the world, plus the respect of his fellow rivals

Bottom left: Jessup in spectacular action for his team, Reading

Bottom centre and bottom right: Jessup displays his talents wearing the colours of England. Jessup first gained international honours in 1970 when he was named in the Young England team to compete against Czechoslovakia and Sweden

He rode best in heats six and eleven, when he had two second places. He was relieved to have made his World Final debut and not too unhappy at his performance, but speedway has a quaint knack of knocking down even the superstars and in 1975, and again in 1976, Jessup failed to reach the World Final.

In 1975 Jessup set the British league alight and zoomed up to almost eleven points a match average. On that form he was one of the favourites to go on from the British final at Coventry to his second World Final, but Jessup had one of the most disastrous nights of his career. Nothing would go right. He finished, a demoralised man with just six points and out of the big chase.

Jessup will never forget the start to 1976. His wife Vicky presented him with a bouncing baby boy, David John, he won a trial and he sought a transfer from Leicester. He had decided that the travel from his Medway, Kent, home to Leicester every week was too much and asked for a transfer to a nearer track.

After the wrangling had finished Jessup went to Reading – for a record transfer fee of £4500. There he became captain and replaced the former Reading number one Anders Michanek, who had retired from British league racing. Michanek's were big shoes indeed for Jessup to fill, but fill them he did and he was soon Reading's favourite rider. He waltzed through the qualifying rounds of the world championship and made it once again to Coventry for the British final. From the British final the top five went through to the Inter-Continental final. Unfortunately Coventry once again turned out to be the end of the road for Jessup's World Final aspirations. He finished sixth, which only gave him reserve place for the next round. Jessup was pipped at the post by John Louis, who won his last race and went through, one point clear of Jessup.

Jessup was an established England star who helped his country reach heady heights in international team competition. He had been a regular in the England World Team Cup squad and had ridden in the World Pairs. His outstanding track talent had given him a win in the prestige Laurels meeting held each year at Wimbledon and notable among the many individual titles he had held were the London Riders championship and the Golden Helmet match race championship.

One thing above all stood out about Jessup. He was the Mr Nice Guy of British speedway. He always had been a quiet, unassuming personality, easy to get along with. He had made as many fans with his easy going manner as he had done with his spectacular riding.   AE

Below: Dave Jessup, riding for the Reading team, fights to hold the lead from Barry Briggs on the inside. Jessup has been a regular Reading rider and has also represented England on a number of different occasions

Man of destiny

If you are a believer in the power of destiny look no further than this Swedish motocross star to prove your case because at some time, somewhere, it was written that Ake Jonsson should never be a world champion. Looking back over his career it is uncanny the number of times he was almost there only to suffer disastrous luck at the eleventh hour. The first year he competed in the World Series was 1968 and he led the championship table after only eight rounds. This naturally caused a great sensation for it is not easy to step into the world circus and win at a first attempt. Jonsson at this time was riding a Husqvarna. Then, over the remaining four grands prix he slipped from the lead to finish the season in third place. However it was an encouraging debut and good enough to catch the eye of Maico, the West German manufacturer, who signed him for the following year.

It could have been the change of mount or overconfidence but 1969 was as bad as 1968 had been good. Sadly Jonsson could only manage to take fifteenth place in the title chase. 1970 was a totally different story. After a modest start to the season he began picking up plenty of points from regular second and third places as the championship wore on into the high summer. At the twelfth and final round, three men were capable of taking the title – all from Sweden. Leading with 80 points was Arne Kring, second was the reigning champion Bengt Aberg on 76 points and third, only four points in arrears, came Ake Jonsson. The last grand prix was the Luxembourg event, held at the Ettelbruck circuit, a tortuous track in a dusty, natural amphitheatre where the temperature can soar up to the 100 degree mark by mid-afternoon.

It was a winner takes all situation. As the 25 starters lined up at the gate Jonsson's spark plug became oiled and his engine stopped. He lifted the machine over the gate and shouted for his mechanic to change it. Tension mounted as Ake once more took his place on the line. The gate fell and the field roared away down the straight but suddenly the Swede was off – an unknown Bulgarian rider had rammed him. 'I don't know what he was doing, he just didn't brake for the corner but came right at me,' Jonsson explained later. There was still a 45-minute race to run though, so, although now last, he set off to catch his competitors. It was then that Jonsson noticed the machine behaving in an unusual manner. Earlier in the day it had been decided to change the front forks after a practice session.

Below: Ake Jonsson (Maico) attempting to overtake Jiri Kavan's CZ on the outside during the 1972 Luxembourg 500cc Grand Prix

The mechanic who did the swop had failed to tighten the upper fork clamp bolts and the twisty course made no allowances for such an omission. To Ake's credit he kept going and had managed to get into fourth place but it was destined for him not to finish the race. On the twelfth lap his 390cc Maico coughed and spluttered to a halt – out of petrol. Unknown to the Swedish star the collision which had occurred in the opening minutes of the race had split the glassfibre tank which meant that for poor Jonsson it was only a matter of time before he discovered his misfortune. With Kring side-lined on medical grounds Aberg retained his title.

One year and eleven grands prix later saw Ake Jonsson in an almost identical situation. After a season-long tussle with the Belgian Roger De Coster, he came to the final round of the World

500cc Motocross Championship with a mere handful of points separating him from the Suzuki man. The season had been a bitter fight for the title both men wanted so badly. It even involved some

Above: Ake Jonsson wears the laurel wreath after winning the 1973 Dutch 500cc Motocross Grand Prix at the famous St Anthonis course

Left: Jonsson in action on the powerful 400cc works Yamaha in 1975

Below: Ake Jonsson (Yamaha) holds off Pierre Karsmakers during the 1975 Dutch 500cc Motocross Grand Prix. By 1975, however, Jonsson's hopes of ever winning a world title were fading. The closest that Jonsson ever got to winning a world crown came in 1970 and '71 but in both cases he was finally pipped at the post

nasty accusations when De Coster claimed Jonsson was getting aid from other Maico riders who were adopting spoiler tactics (not riding to win but to hinder the opposition). The last grand prix for 1971 was the Dutch, held at the famous course at St Anthonis where the deep sand resembled a beach rather than a motocross track. In practice Jonsson was the faster man but De Coster had been training in sand at Mol and Lummel and planned to let the Swede make the pace. All eyes were on the two leading contenders as the first race got under way but then on the first lap Jonsson slowed down and eventually stopped. The reserve spark plug on his machine had unscrewed causing a complete loss of compression. Was there ever a more miserable sight than Ake standing astride his silent bike watching De Coster go past on his way to his first World Championship?

Still he would not admit defeat. A mechanic replaced the plug and although a lap down Ake set off to do what he could – he finished tenth. Showing true grit in the second race he stormed into the lead and stayed there, forcing De Coster to take runner-up spot but it was academic because Roger knew that battle was over, the glory was his while the gallantry was Jonsson's. Less than a month later the Scandinavian was to get his sweet revenge when at the Moto Cross des Nations in France – an event involving both the 250 and 500 World Championship riders – he took first place in both races. Onlookers could not help smiling when only a few minutes before the start Jonsson was seen in the pits tightening his spark plugs.

Ake was born in October 1942 at Vasteras in Sweden where, in 1977, he still lives with his wife and two children. When not competing in motocross he likes to ice-skate. In fact, he is something of a local hero on the blades because he has won no less than ten ice-skating championships in and around his home town. He also became a writer when he teamed with the American free-lance journalist Vin Gilligan to produce a book called *The Techniques of Moto Cross*. He became a professional rider in 1967 and since then has regularly taken positions in the top ten in the World Championships including two seconds, two thirds and a fourth. He has ridden Husqvarna, Maico and Yamaha and although fated never to become a world title holder he has nevertheless left an indelible mark for it is often said that it is not the way the winner wins but the way the loser loses which makes motocross an entertaining sport. Surely Ake Jonsson, will bear witness to that . **RB**

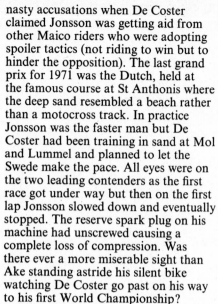

When your job was that of testing the most powerful racing machines in the world, it followed that you would make a pretty formidable rider in the heat of top competition. That was exactly how it turned out for Japanese rider Hideo Kanaya, 32 years old in 1977, and who had been Yamaha's top racing tester for several years. It was only during the mid-1970s that Japanese riders really came to the fore in World Championship racing – particularly in the large-capacity classes – and, by 1977, two, Kanaya and Takazumi Katayama, were among the best in the world.

Hideo amazed European fans and riders alike in 1972 when he won the first European race he entered, the 250cc event at the West German Grand Prix. After scoring well in other Grands Prix, he went back to Japan to continue development work on the bikes that were to shatter the world in the following year, a 250cc two-stroke twin developing more than 55bhp and weighing less than 220lb, and also a 500cc, water-cooled two-stroke four producing twice the power of its smaller sister and beating the until then dominant Italian MV Augusta. It was Yamaha's big works team return, following a four year lay-off from the days of Phil Read, the late Bill Ivy and

Above: Kanaya after winning the 1975 500cc Austrian Grand Prix

Below: Hideo Kanaya leads Patrick Fernandez and Bruno Kneubuhler, at the 250cc Dutch Grand Prix

TESTER EXTRAORDINAIRE

their unbeatable four-cylinder, two-stroke racers.

The 1973 Yamahas were ridden by Hideo and Jarno Saarinen, the flying Finn who dominated the World Championship in both categories until he was killed in a pile-up at Monza. Before that, Kanaya had ridden to second and third places in the 250cc and 500cc races respectively at the French Grand Prix, and also finished second in both 250cc and 500cc races at the Austrian Grand Prix.

For a spell after the Monza incident, Yamaha kept a low profile out of respect for Saarinen but, in that dramatic World Championship sortie, Kanaya had learned a lot, both about the bikes he was helping to develop and about his own riding techniques. In the following three years, those skills made him one of the most respected Japanese opponents on the circuits.

Kanaya first came to the notice of the Western press when he became the Japanese 350cc champion in 1971, and

he began his vital work with Yamaha in 1972, when he was just 27. In 1975 and 1976, the 9½-stone, 5ft 6in tall rider became a regular world championship contestant again, riding as team-mate to Yamaha's new number one rider, Giacomo Agostini.

1974 was a disastrous year for the Japanese ace, for he crashed heavily in the Daytona 200-miler in Florida and, as a result, missed that year's Grand Prix season. He rounded that year off well, however, by finishing second overall in the All Japan Road Race Grand Prix.

Unfortunately, Hideo tended to fall off his machine a bit more often than most. Always a daring rider, particularly in the big-money, ultra-fast Daytona classic, he was regularly in the hunt for the leading positions, but he never made it to the winners' rostrum there.

Away from America, however, was a different story. Kanaya, whose home town was Kobe, Hyogoken, Japan, gained the 90cc Japanese championship in addition to the 350cc home title in 1971. He also made a fairy tale World Championship debut at the 1972 West German Grand Prix, when he also came second in the 350cc class. He went on to take second place in the 350cc race at the Austrian Grand Prix that year, then third in the 500cc class at the Belgian Grand Prix.

In 1975, Kanaya – who, like many of his countrymen was a keen golfer – finished third in the 500cc World championship, scoring 45 points against team-mate Agostini's 84 and runner-up Phil Read's 76 with his MV Agusta.

The Japanese ace also played a leading role in the development of the formidable Yamaha OW31 750cc four-cylinder two-strokes, as ridden by top Americans Steve Baker and Kenny Roberts. Here, he helped to break new ground with the use of more efficient streamlinings and the use of cantilever rear suspension arrangements.

Even so, poor Hideo's reputation for falling off tended to grow on him. At one point, he seemed to suffer spills almost every time he went out to race, and at the Venezuelan Grand Prix in 1976 he came to grief twice. Kanaya was, however, one of the most resilient riders in the business, and just kept bouncing back.

In 1977, he went back to Japan, and became engaged in a lot of further development work in Yamaha's competition department – working on something sensational to beat the all-conquering four-cylinder racers being produced by the rival Suzuki factory.

Whenever he could find the time, however, Hideo continued to race in Far East events like the Singapore Grand Prix, and he still had a lot of top-level racing in front of him as the 1977 season drew to a close.   PK

Below: Japan's ace tester Hideo Kanaya competing in the 1976 Venezuelan Formula 750 Grand Prix on his works OW31 Yamaha, a machine he helped to develop

The perfect candidate

When Pierre Karsmakers turned his back on European motocross to ride regularly in the United States, he left behind his chance of winning a world title. The world series, substantially Europe-based, had years of tradition behind it and Karsmakers himself agreed that it was still the greatest series. But the American dream which drew him to the United States in 1973 was tempting: and his consolation – if consolation he was likely to need! – was that he became one of the highest paid motocross superstars in the world.

Dutch-born Karsmakers, three times national motocross champion of Holland and with a solid racing background of nine years, was in at the start of the remarkable motocross popularity explosion which hit the United States towards the mid 1970s. Impressed by the way Karsmakers, along with other Europeans, had shown American riders the way home during the international TransAMA series, Yamaha US team head Pete Schick asked the Dutchman what he thought about racing in American motocross.

Schick wanted someone like Karsmakers to show the young Americans the ropes. Not only did he have the experience and ability, but spoke several languages and was a great ambassador for the sport. He was the perfect candidate. From then, early in 1973, Karsmakers was on his way to becoming a motocross superstar and in 36 US starts through the season, collected overall honours 17 times and won the National Open Championship.

Pierre Karsmakers, for all his glamour image, is a tough competitor. Schick said he was the toughest person on equipment he had seen, a statement borne out by the rider's own belief that to win at the sport you have to ride your machine so hard it is completely worn out at the finish. In fact while with Yamaha he asked them to build a machine to his own specifications because he felt the factory bikes weren't strong enough. His knowledge of suspensions and engineering came from a college engineering degree and he proved he knew what he was talking

about by taking the Yamaha, with an all-new frame built to his own specifications, to victory in the TransAMA 1974 final at Carlsbad, California.

By 1975 the American motocross boom was well established with two-day shows attracting crowds of 45,000 and more, and races fiercely contested by as many as ten fully-supported factory teams including Honda, Yamaha, Suzuki and Kawasaki. Yamaha had done much to push the boom along, jumping on the publicity bandwagon with a superseries of events and other activities; and making Karsmakers, in the process, into a top celebrity.

But by 1975, Karsmakers had left Yamaha for a rich two-year contract dangled temptingly by Honda. The popularity of motocross in the United States had been accompanied by a phenomenal growth in the sale of motocross and off-road machines and Honda wanted Karsmakers to spearhead their activity in the sport as a means of capturing a higher share of the expanding market. The high

Overleaf: Dutchman Pierre Karsmakers jumps his fire-engine-red Honda during a motocross meeting in America held in 1976. Karsmakers was one of the first Europeans to race in the USA and, on realising the financial advantages of racing in America, left his native Holland to settle in the States. He was then signed by Yamaha, and later by Honda, and was largely responsible for helping motocross to develop in America

This page: three views of Karsmakers in action on a Yamaha, for whom he rode during 1973, '74 and '77

contesting about the same number of races, he was based at home for most of the time, jetted to meetings with all expenses paid, and enjoyed the luxury of two factory mechanics to look after his machines.

He enjoyed all the trappings of super-stardom and while his contract guaranteed him a win-or-lose sum, he claimed it was still the results he cared most about. 'If you don't win, what's the point of racing?'

This kind of professionalism won Karsmakers, who has enriched motocross in America, many friends. He was relentlessly hard-working. In 1975 his Honda holed a piston at one meeting, threw a chain in another. He was so worried that 48 hours later he was on a jet for Japan. The next ten days were spent at the Honda factory, testing six different prototypes for eight and a half hours a day.

While still giving priority to American motocross, Honda decided in the end to contest a number of Grand Prix events in 1975 and Karsmakers, after scoring three second places in American and Canadian rounds of the 500cc championship, was sent to Hawkstone Park in Britain where, on bikes which arrived direct from Japan, he notched a fifth place. The exercise was said to be part of Honda's development programme to test their bikes in Europe against world-class opposition.

In 1976 Honda took the first major step towards what looked like a serious challenge in Grand Prix competition, sending the colourful Karsmakers over to Switzerland, where he scored fourth highest points in the first round of the 500cc world championship. He finished the season in ninth position and towards the end of the year, amid rumours that Honda would mount from Japan a world championship motocross invasion, Karsmakers was strongly tipped for team leadership.

But then came the shock news that American Brad Lackey had been signed for their world 500cc title bid. Karsmakers, his two-year contract having run its course, switched to Yamaha and during 1977 rode as team-mate to Heikki Mikkola, back on the world championship trail.

But his European venture was to end in frustration and in July, after chipping a wrist, he quit Europe for 1977 and returned to the United States to contest the 500cc motocross championship series there. Further Grand Prix involvement is on the cards, however, for no matter how lucrative American motocross might be to Karsmakers, one has the feeling that a world title, for him, is a world title after all . . . and that is an honour he would like. **PC**

standard of living in America meant more motor cycles were being sold there than overseas and an American motocross championship, in commercial terms, was more important to Honda than the world series. So Karsmakers contract tied him exclusively to racing in America, which he had dominated since his arrival, and coincided with Honda's introduction of new bikes, including a 360cc two-stroke and an experimental four-stroke, for a major effort in the American open class championship.

After moving with his wife and children to his newly adopted home in southern California, Pierre Karsmakers life-style changed dramatically. Before moving from Europe he would compete in some 40 races a year in perhaps ten countries: and to make more than £6000 a year, after expenses, he would have to be his own manager, mechanic, sponsor and drive himself to and from race meetings.

His Honda contract was said to be worth about £30,000 and while

Japan's Rising Son

Europe included a GP win in Sweden and this scintillating form had come only four years after his introduction to the sport.

His first love for racing, however, was formed around the world of racing cars. He took up sports car racing with his elder brother when he first got the taste for speed but soon gave up, for his burning desire to become a champion, he knew, would be easier to fulfil in the world of motor cycle racing.

His ambition to become a car racer came when he left school at the age of 17. It was at school that he learned to speak English although his delivery today in the European paddocks still has a heavy oriental accent.

Disillusioned with the prospects of becoming a budding champion on four wheels, Takazumi Katayama took to two wheels in 1971 – on a 250cc Yamaha. Success was almost instant for the teenager whose fascination for motor cycles had started on the streets with illegal rides around his home city of Kobe, 350 miles from the seaport of Tokyo.

As a works rider in Japan he collected his country's 250cc title in 1972 and the 350cc title a year later. His team was then a luxurious set up with all machines provided and two

Left: a perplexed Takazumi Katayama pictured at Brands Hatch in 1976

Below: Katayama in action at Brands on his Yamaha

Japanese road racer Takazumi Katayama made history in 1977 when he became the first person from his country to win a world championship. The popular pop star turned racer won the 350cc title in convincing style with a clinching victory at the Imatra circuit in Finland.

His title win is of great significance to the Far East. Despite the undoubted engineering and technical talents of the Japanese manufacturers, they have never had a champion to boast. Before 'Zooming Taxi', as he is affectionately known, became 350 title holder, the Japanese factories had earned riders 35 world titles in the thirteen years leading up to 1973 and a further 38 manufacturers awards.

When Katayama first arrived in Europe in 1974 his sole intention was to get that desperately wanted title for his homeland and his first performances, with a fourth in the 250 championship of that year, showed he wasn't far away from his goal. His successes during that first year in

mechanics for the nine road race circuits in Japan. Before he left for Europe he was also given the opportunity to test the then new TZ750 Yamaha now the most common of superbikes throughout the world.

His potential for the European circus became obvious with his frequent beating of Yamaha's earlier Japanese ambassador to Europe, Hideo Kanaya. These performances earned him the title 'Prince of Speed'. Following his explosive introduction to Europe he was never out of the news. His efforts in the world championships have always been impressive and his success in 1977 was by no means unwarranted.

In 1977 he rode under the Sarome banner with team mate Chas Mortimer although the bulk of his help came from the European Yamaha headquarters in Amsterdam. He had been actively involved with the development of a 350cc three-cylinder Yamaha engine which he used during his campaign in 1977.

Katayama is an amazingly determined rider and his visit to the Isle of Man in 1976 illustrated this quality in him. On his first visit to the demanding $37\frac{3}{4}$ mile course he put in a superb performance in the 250cc TT to finish just 26 seconds behind winner Tom Herron. This was without doubt one of the most impressive performances during TT week in modern times.

Through his involvement in GP racing Katayama has made many friends and is renowned throughout Europe for his happy disposition. He has a characteristic huge grin, pleasant personality and is always ready to laugh. Of his rivals he especially rated South Africans Alan North and Kork Ballington and had a special word of praise for Ulsterman Tom Herron.

With one world title under his belt he was planning to defend it in 1978 but he also wanted to add to his solitary world crown. In 1978 he planned to concentrate again on the 250 and 350cc classes but after clinching the 1977 350cc crown announced that he would also be moving up to 500cc level. His main challenger throughout 1977 would be to take world 500cc champion Barry Sheene's title away from him. He hoped that Yamaha would provide him with a four-cylinder 500cc machine but if not would buy his own 500cc Suzuki with which to go after world championship points.   AM

Below: Takazumi Katayama hurls his Yamaha TZ750 through Paddock Bend during the 1976 Hutchinson 100 held at Brands Hatch

The Sign of the Big K

Japan's post-war commercial and industrial miracle for the making and selling of motor cycles throughout the world had already materialised when Kawasaki began to move into focus in the 1960s. Honda had more than ten years start, Suzuki and Yamaha were already dominant, and Kawasaki needed to be different to be noticed. With commendable insight and marketing instinct, it rapidly built a reputation for high performance bikes with remarkable acceleration and outstanding enthusiast appeal.

The factory's first racing appearance was in 1965 when it produced an array of 125cc two-stroke fours and water cooled twins fitted with two rotary valves on the starting grid of the Japanese Grand Prix. It is likely that the performance was a disappointment to the factory chiefs, for the machines were not seen in force again. British champion of 1965, Dave Simmonds was entrusted with one but when put to the test in Grand Prix events, failed miserably. Competition was too fierce in the class and there was little hope of Simmons taking the title while Yamaha and Suzuki continued to run officially; but once they departed, the Kawasaki was almost unbeatable and Simmons brought them their first world championship in 1969 on a machine which was virtually unchanged from 1966, yet still developed 30bhp at 14,000rpm and could reach 118mph.

The origins of Kawasaki go back to 1878 when Shozo Kawasaki started a dockyard in Tokyo. This later developed into the manufacture of locomotives, railway coaches, freight cars, bridge trusses and steel. In 1937, the Kawasaki Aircraft Company was formed and it was this development which in time led

Left: Kawasaki built their reputation on the phenomenal performance of their 500cc three-cylinder two-stroke machine. This is the 1969 model being accelerated away from standstill. Because of its narrow power band and light weight, it was easy to lift the front wheel

885

Kawasaki into motor cycle production.

The organisation had a base of high technology and when the aircraft company found itself wanting to diversify, following a decline in business after the war, they turned to the making of motor cycle engines.

By the early 1950s they were supplying 58cc two-stroke units and 148cc overhead valve singles to various manufacturers to be sold under several brand names, including Meihatsu, made by Meihatsu Heavy Industries, a Kawasaki subsidiary.

After Honda introduced their open-framed 'nifty-fifty' in 1959, the motor cycle revolution which was already on its way took off in spectacular fashion and Kawasaki was poised to move more deeply into the business. In 1961 the Meihatsu concern was reorganised to become Kawasaki Auto Sales and after opening a brand new development and mass production assembly plant in Kobe, planned largely by the aircraft company, the Meihatsu marque was dropped to make way for a Kawasaki identity of its own. The Meguro Manufacturing Company, Japan's oldest motor cycle manufacturer who were finding the rapidly changing and highly competitive world increasingly difficult to live with, was taken over by Kawasaki that same year, giving marketing rights, through Kawasaki outlets, of the Meguro ohv twins throughout Japan and south-east Asia under the Kawasaki-Meguro name. This gave Kawasaki the chance, later in 1961, to move into production with a full range of motor cycles from 50cc to 500cc.

The first motor cycle to carry the Kawasaki name exclusively was produced in 1962 – a 125cc two-stroke street machine called the B8. The following year the first Kawasaki motocross model, the B8M, was developed and produced.

Nineteen sixty-nine was a significant year for the young company. Not only did Kawasaki win that 125cc world title, but there was important reorganisation of company groupings, the merging of three subsidiary companies creating Kawasaki Heavy Industries Ltd with the brief to advance and develop their motor cycle interests. The year also saw the introduction of the now famous Kawasaki H1, a two-stroke, three-cylinder 500cc machine which was to consolidate the Kawasaki image for high performance motor cycles. Many regard it to be the first true modern generation superbike and it was produced specifically as a performance machine.

Almost from the start, Kawasaki saw their progress charted in the graph of overseas sales, with the vast potential of the United States a priority target. Their modern range was keyed closely to the demands of the North American market, and their much respected models were later strongly supported by a large

collection of motocross and enduro machines to capitalise on the popularity explosion of off-road sport in America.

Their first overseas office was set up in Chicago in 1965 primarily to supply parts and, to a limited degree, distribute the M10 50cc machines. Shortly after, Kawasaki were able to offer a wide range of lightweights on the American market – 90, 100, 120 and 125cc machines, topped by the Model A1 250cc Samurai twin, which achieved reasonable success in America but faired less well in Europe. It was significant, however, because from the Samurai was derived the 125cc road-race model first ridden by Toshio Fuji in 1966, and which in turn led to Simmonds' capture of the world title. Kawasaki also recognised the growing importance of the European market with the setting up of a massive parts complex, formed as a directly-owned subsidiary of the parent company in Japan. The establishment of directly owned subsidiaries was to become part of Kawasaki's 'space-age'

Above: the 1967 Kawasaki A1SS used a 250cc twin-cylinder, disc-valve engine which developed 31bhp at 8000rpm

strategy and over the years took the place of local concessionaires in many areas, the United States and Britain included.

By about the middle 1970s, Kawasaki were exporting motor cycles to ninety different countries from their Akashi works near Kobe in Japan. Originally built in 1930 for the production of aircraft parts, the plant maintained very high rates in the production of motor cycles, employing some 1700 people for an annual output of 250,000 bikes. A milestone in the company's history was reached at Lincoln, Nebraska, USA, when at 10am on 22 January 1975, the first Kawasaki motor cycle to be manufactured in the United States rolled off the assembly line . . . a KZ400. Representing an investment of about £7 million (1975 values), the plant originally covered 270,000 square feet and was the first full

scale production unit to be established by any Japanese manufacturer outside Japan.

After having established their first overseas office in the United States in 1965, only five years after producing their first motor cycle, Kawasaki closed it down a year later, on the formation of Kawasaki Motors Inc with headquarters in Los Angeles and this gave way to Kawasaki Motors Corporation, in 1968, with headquarters at Santa Ana, California.

Kawasaki in the United States point to the willingness of the parent company in Japan to leave them very much on their own to work out their own future as a major reason for the impressive strides made by the company in America. Kawasaki in America claim that it did not have to be sensitive to the established policy, customs and traditions of the Japanese parent company and that much of the success of Kawasaki in America was because it was not part of Japan Inc, but a consumer orientated company. By 1977, Kawasaki was the largest American motor cycle producer and in 1976 sold 150,000 units to collect a brand share of 17 per cent.

The European market was seen as second in importance only to America and in 1974, the setting up of the huge parts complex in Holland was the start of a careful process of greater concentration in one market after another where they had originally set up concessionaire agreements, with wholly-owned subsidiaries taking over in Germany (1975) and Australia, in addition to Britain and America.

In Britain, the Kawasaki subsidiary was established in February 1974 and was the springboard to a programme of intense activity and concentration.

By the early 1970s, Kawasaki's export trade was running at an impressive 80 per cent of total production, with the parent company in Japan, through subsidiaries, intent on streamlining the entire supply routine, from the assembly line to dealers showrooms.

Promoting strongly its high-performance image, Kawasaki was active in motor cycle racing and as early as 1968 was winning events near home like the 350cc class of the Singapore Grand Prix and races in Kuala Lumpar. They dominated the field at the first All-Japan cross country races and in the Japanese Moto-

G. Betti

Opposite page, bottom: a 500cc Kawasaki triple of the mid-1970s; this refined version was a far cry from the early Mach III s

Above: the 500cc H1 model of 1968; this version of the Mach III differs from later models in that it has drum brakes on the front wheel

cross Grand Prix of 1968, gained first and second places in the 90cc event, first and third in the 125cc event and second and third in the 250cc class.

That same year saw the beginning of Kawasaki's American race effort, when the twin 250cc dual rotary valve Samurai became the A1-racer in the hands of Ralph White and Walt Fulton. It was a modest beginning in terms of success, but it led the following year to a courageous performance by Dick Hammer as he raced the 350cc A7R against the might of other factory 750s. Fulton, with Art Baumann and Cal Rayborn, raced improved 250s and all bikes finished in the top ten in their class at Daytona in 1969.

Unlike the other Japanese factories, Kawasaki rejected the idea of building exotic machines purely for factory racing. They claimed their policy was to start with stock machines, improve them, race them, win with them if they could, and put them back into production for the public to use. When Brad Lackey's 450cc F12 won the US motocross championship the company proudly announced that it was built for the public and was not a super esoteric works machine nobody would ever see off the race track.

Kawasaki's racing really began with the introduction of the famous 500cc H1, after the factory had made it into a racer. Replicas designated the H1R, were snapped up and racing one of them, French-Canadian Yvon Du Hamel won the first AMA national championship for Kawasaki in 1971, in the process lifting the average speed for a 250-mile race to 108mph. The Kawasaki was the first 500cc racer to be offered for sale by a major motor cycle manufacturer for ten years, and with a claimed output of 75bhp and a top speed of 150mph, it made a big impact. It did have its critics, however, because the machine had a high centre of gravity which made it difficult for short circuit events. But it accelerated the advance of the two-stroke in 500cc racing and, in Grand Prix events, Ginger Molloy rode Kawasaki to good effect. With second places to the mighty MV of Agostini in France, Finland, Ireland and Spain, he ended the season runner-up in the world championship.

The 500 led, logically, to the 750cc H2 Mach 1V superbike. This inevitably became the H2R which, ridden by Yvon Du Hamel, Paul Smart and Gary Nixon in 1972, gave Kawasaki a magnificent season, Du Hamel yet again creating a new record speed while winning the Talladega 200, reputed to be America's fastest race, at an average of 110.44mph on his Team Hansen machine. Nixon and Smart finished second and fourth. Kawasaki had moved swiftly following Bob Hansen's split with Honda and signed him up to organise their racing effort.

In motocross, which increased its

Top: one of Kawasaki's famous two-stroke, three-cylinder machines of the 1960s, this being the 350cc model

Above: this is a Z900 Kawasaki of the mid 1970s. It was a direct descendant of the famous Z1 model

popularity so dramatically in America in the 1970s, Kawasaki also had a good performance record. The first off-road machines were built in 1970 – 173cc, 250cc and 350cc enduros. In late 1971 the big 450cc F12 was launched purely for motocross. With this machine Brad Lackey captured the AMA motocross championship in 1972 and Kawasaki was to add further to its prestige when celebrated American rider Jim Weinert secured the AMA national open class championship in 1974 to give the factory a second championship in three seasons.

Again, in 1976 the same rider brought Kawasaki the AMA supercross series.

Kawasaki prides itself, not entirely without justification, on manufacturing the 'today motor cycle' and certainly in its comparatively short history the company has demonstrated a well developed feel for progress and innovation along carefully planned lines. Technically, Kawasaki machines are highly sophisticated and the factory helped to pioneer such advances as electronic ignition and full instrumentation. They did much towards achieving progress through such

Top left: The roller-bearing 903cc engine is famous for its smoothness and even power delivery

Top right: The 398cc Z400 four-stroke engine which produced 36bhp at 8500rpm.

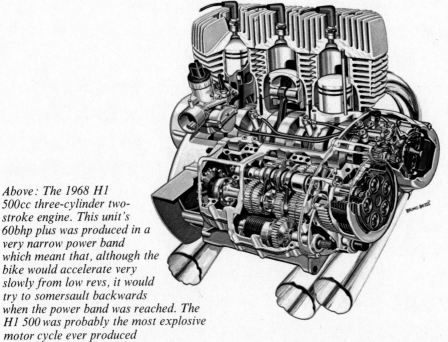

Above: The 1968 H1 500cc three-cylinder two-stroke engine. This unit's 60bhp plus was produced in a very narrow power band which meant that, although the bike would accelerate very slowly from low revs, it would try to somersault backwards when the power band was reached. The H1 500 was probably the most explosive motor cycle ever produced

give the proper degree of back-up service to its customers and build up the close liaison with dealers which is an essential part of the firms' marketing strategy.

Indeed, when the British subsidiary started operating, many regarded it as an act of utter irresponsibility and folly that they rejected the dealership network already available through the concessionaire arrangement and began once more to build up carefully from scratch on an 'exclusive' basis. Dealer saturation and discount selling techniques, it was claimed, led to bazaar images with low site investment and poor display, and over-concentration on a quick turnover. The company stated publicly that it did not want to market on these terms where long range considerations were being sacrificed in short term gains by manufacturers and dealers alike.

In machine terms, its achievements have largely centred around the introduction of the H1 in 1969, a three-cylinder 500cc machine with exceptional performance and acceleration, and in 1972 of the now famous 900cc Z1. Back in 1967, Kawasaki had already brought out the biggest capacity machine ever produced in Japan, the 650W, its first four-cylinder machine, but although the bike had ridden the years well, the Kawasaki hierarchy realised something new was required to carry the company into the 1970s and to provide a big brother for its successful 500.

So Kawasaki set to work on a new 750 superbike and planned to back it with as much modern technology and up-to-date marketing as could be mustered. After much research – in the United States market particularly – the company decided it wanted a powerful touring bike incorporating good handling characteristics and high mechanical standards; it had to be well equipped and, because of the environmental laws in America, as pollution-free as possible. Under the code name New York Steak, the boffins set to work on the four-cylinder, double-overhead-camshaft 750cc machine. But unknown to Kawasaki, Honda had been working on an almost identical project and got its new bike to the market first, unveiling the CB750 at the Tokyo Show in October 1968. It was a savage blow to Kawasaki's hopes, but a year was spent looking at the impact of the Honda 750, seeing if the market could stand a competitor. The decision was taken to go ahead with the original project . . . but to produce a 900cc version of the 750.

The first engines had problems in the oil system, a malfunction of the crankcase breather arrangement causing engine oil to spray out, but one of the prototypes developed over 95hp and in a test run clocked an impressive 141mph.

In February 1972, a couple of prototype Z1s were sent to America for testing

developments as smoother, vibration-free running, efficient silencing and pollution-free exhaust emission. And in competition technique, the rotary inlet valve was adapted by the Japanese industry, especially Kawasaki, for the two-stroke motor. They also have a highly developed sense of marketing and sales values and probably invested more heavily during the early 1970s in researching the market than did any other manufacturer.

The firm makes no secret of its aim in going into racing: to gain 'brand awareness' which, indeed, it could be said was

a reason for them moving into motor cycles in the first place; for Kawasaki, although a massive organisation employing more than 30,000 people, had little point of public recognition. Nobody knew who the company was. That, also, accounts partially for its entrepreneurial approach. It projects a commercial flair which finds expression in such attitudes as an insistence (in Britain certainly – and also in America in intent) – on establishing dealerships. It believes that only in this way, as manufacturers of performance bikes, can it

and broke a number of records and the machines, before being returned to Japan, were test ridden across the American continent and around various courses and circuits en route, covering a total distance of almost 12,500 miles, without trouble.

The Z1 was announced at the Cologne Motor Show in 1972 and in 1973 a production Z1 set a new world 24-hour speed and endurance record at Daytona. The machine became the flagship of the Kawasaki range and in succeeding years, with the 1000cc machine which followed, was to win 'Bike of the Year' awards in many countries and perform with distinction in long distance endurance races such as the prestigious Bol d'Or.

Kawasaki racing activity contributed much to the European scene, as well as in America, during the mid 1970s. Kawasaki UK, a wholly-owned subsidiary, was set up in 1974 in the twilight gloom of Britain's crisis-ridden three-day working week. John Norman, taken on by Kawasaki after experience with BMW and particularly Honda, master-minded, with his Japanese superiors, the British operation, often by candlelight, from their one-room office headquarters in London's Holiday Inn. By 1977, the firm's headquarters was a smart, modern, purpose-built unit conveniently located near to London at Slough.

The charisma which had been part of Kawasaki's deliberate American plan was carried into Europe and, in racing terms, centred around the performance of the 'Green Meanies'. Lime green and white were chosen as racing colours because green, possibly reflecting its ill-luck suggestions, had been ignored or rejected by other racers; so in green, Kawasaki team members and their support crews would be picked out instantly. The 'Green Meanie' tag was completed because, at the time, Kawasaki machines had the reputation for being particularly fast on the straights with exceptional acceleration, but were somewhat 'mean' on the bends.

Below: when Kawasaki's four-cylinder, four-stroke 900cc engine was introduced it did not take enthusiasts long to realise the engine's potential. This is the mighty twin-engined 'Big Spender' drag bike of Holland's Henk Vink

With contract riders Mick Grant and Barry Ditchburn, Team Kawasaki soon became a strong force in motor cycle sport based in Britain. In 1975, the team's first year, Grant set a new lap record on the Isle of Man on the water-cooled KR750 and also won the Senior event on the new KR500. Ditchburn completed record-breaking performances at Silverstone and secured the King of Brands title. Grant was first and Ditchburn second in the British Superbike series that year.

Under team manager Stan Shenton, the racing policy of Kawasaki UK remained remarkably stable, though too often mechanical breakdowns caused retirements when it seemed that nothing could prevent these remarkably fast machines from winning.

Internationally, Kawasaki gave strong support, as expected, to the Formula 750 series of races. Although Kawasaki along with Suzuki and Yamaha, had officially withdrawn its racing effort towards the end of 1975 because of a general fall-off in sales in America and a stockpile of machines, Yamaha approached the first round of the championship series at Daytona in 1976 with a tremendous advantage. Its new 750 OW31 was already built and tested in Japan and four machines were ready for the new season when Yamaha announced its withdrawal. Kawasaki, along with Suzuki, were less fortunate, so while the company had to contest Daytona in 1976 with the previous year's bikes, Yamaha could find no reason for not using its new machines.

Even so, the Kawasaki of Gary Nixon finished second to Cecotto's Yamaha. Although Mick Grant did well to finish third in Belgium and also set the fastest lap at Silverstone (Ditchburn doing the same in Belgium) Nixon was the most successful Kawasaki racer in the series and finished the season in second place.

Kawasaki have also made an important contribution to endurance racing, thanks to a far-sighted move by their French

importer, Xavier Maugendre. Until the return of the classic Bol d'Or to the official racing calendar, towards the end of the 1960s, endurance racing was a little rated and much neglected branch of motor cycle sport. The technical improvements in production machinery, in which Kawasaki undoubtedly played its part, and the emphasis on street bikes in the early 1970s, heralded a new era and a fresh public interest in endurance racing. While the sport had been incapable of attracting the top professional riders on anything other than a very occasional basis, the big names began to move into endurance racing as the FIM Coupe d'Endurance assumed a semi-official status.

Frenchman Georges Godier's professional approach to endurance racing attracted Maugendre's interest and the result of their contact, the formation of the Kawa-Godier SIDEMM team (and its success) brought counter-attacks from BMW and Honda-France. Suddenly, it seemed, endurance racing was big time, attracting spectator interest with crowds of 120,000 for instance at the Bol d'Or.

Through the remarkable combination of Godier and Genoud, Kawasaki won the Bol d'Or in 1974 and '75. In 1974 it also secured second place through Guili and Choukroun, and in 1975 did even better, all three top positions occupied by Kawasaki machines. In 1976, Honda won the race, with Kawasakis in second and third positions. Yvon Du Hamel and Jean-Francois Baldé had teamed for 1976, as they had in 1975 when they took third place, and for the first twelve hours kept the 1000cc Kawasaki in lead position, but their effort faltered in the later stages when problems with the alternator occurred. Kawasaki, however, had the consolation of occupying four of the first seven places and of setting the fastest lap time.

In 1976, three Australian riders from Sydney took a stock standard Kawasaki Z900 round a track for 114 hours to set a new world endurance record: and in Holland, Kawasaki distributor Henk Vink (drag expert and world record holder with a time of 9.02 seconds over the standing start quarter mile using a single engine Kawasaki dragster) unveiled his new machine, an 8-cylinder Kawasaki incorporating two virtually standard 980cc engines with which, in 1977, he clocked an incredible 208mph from a standing start to become the fastest man in the world over the kilometre.

By 1977, however, Kawasaki in the United States had officially pulled out of major racing, although activity through Kawasaki UK remained at a high level. In fact the company declared its determination to go all out for the F750 world title and Barry Ditchburn moved the marque off to an optimistic start with a fine win at Nogaro, France, in March. He rode the latest lightweight factory machine and faced some of Europe's top F750 riders. Grant almost made it a Kawasaki one-two, but the throttle stuck open with only five laps remaining.

During the season, Kawasaki's effort began to falter, although there was plenty of consolation as Mick Grant reflected on what was undoubtedly his most impressive visit to the Isle of Man. In the six laps 1000cc Classic TT, he slashed 5.4s off the outright lap record, setting a new TT race average of 110.76mph as he led the field throughout the race. But perhaps the most interesting development in 1977 was Kawasaki's exploratory contest of the 250cc Grand Prix series. The in-line 250cc two-stroke twin had been brought in during 1975, but suffered severely from vibration, though its light weight and competitive power made it a major potential challenger in the class.

Pre-season testing by Grant and Ditchburn underlined the promise and Australian Gregg Hansford gave it an impressive showing at Daytona. In June, Kawasaki history was made by Mick Grant when he won the 250cc Dutch TT at Assen. His start-to-finish victory was the Kawasaki factory's first 250cc GP success. Grant looked set to reproduce his Dutch TT form eight days later in the Belgian GP, but after rocketing into the lead from the start, he lost ground to finish way down the field. He came back strongly in Sweden, taking the in-line Kawasaki to an impressive victory.

The year was also important for Kawasaki for in March the factory indulged in a successful bout of record breaking at Daytona following the big meeting.

In a way Kawasaki is unique among the major Japanese manufacturers. Honda look back on a traditional success story, from a small shack in war-torn Tokyo to the biggest motor cycle organisation the world has known. A recession in textiles forced Suzuki to look around for other means of support and they followed Honda's example into motor cycles. Yamaha moved into the industry after being world famous for reed organs and pianos.

Kawasaki is different in that it was already a vast organisation with an enormous spread of technological expertise when it moved into the production of motor cycles and, the company would claim, brought along engineering

Inset: Kawasaki rider Mick Grant leans his three-cylinder 750 into the hairpin at Mallory Park

Right: Grant in action on the twin-cylinder 250cc racer at Silverstone during 1977

credentials which go far beyond those of its major competitors. In 1977, Kawasaki built turbine, diesel and jet engines, locomotives, rolling stock, buses, small engines, generators, heavy duty vehicle equipment, helicopters, jet aircraft; and motor cycles. It also constructed industrial and chemical plant, bridges and steel structures, anti-pollution systems and nuclear equipment.

While in motor cycling the company presents a dynamic image, essential to such an exciting industry, it also manages to convey the impression of a company which has worked out carefully in advance exactly what it is attempting to achieve and seems disinterested in action by impulse. It holds in respect the modern philosophy of responsible and planned marketing.

For the all-out racing enthusiast, of course, Kawasaki is frustrating because it had not, by 1977, made a full-blooded assault on the prestigious Grand Prix events. Perhaps it recognised the 750 class and endurance racing as a more sensible way of gaining recognition, in view of its product range being biased as it is towards high value, high capacity, performance motor cycles.

But there are exciting and encouraging trends. Kawasaki's contact in 1977 with classic racing in the 250cc class, particularly in view of the Grand Prix rounds' continued popularity, must be looked upon as a step in the right direction. Although some of the results were no doubt disappointing for Kawasaki in the early part of the 1977 season, there is every chance that it will persist in its racing policy which so far has done much to give that essential point of public recognition.

In fact, reports were circulated that Kawasaki would step up its involvement in racing during 1978. Race department officials who came to Europe from Japan were said to have gone home happy with the progress made during 1977. Having moved into 250cc events in 1977, a 350cc version of the 250 would seem a likely move from which the Kawasaki name would enjoy additional exposure.

What many would really like to see, of course, is a Kawasaki competing in the 500cc world championships, since the company could provide a new challenge to the dominance of Suzuki. Will it ever happen? Maybe Kawasaki itself would find it difficult to answer that one, but one thing is certain: if it felt it was right to do it, the firm would do it.

And the challenge would be no greater than the one it willingly accepted when it moved into motor cycling's big league less than a decade ago.

Left: Torleif Hansen in action on his Kawasaki during the 1977 British 250cc Motocross Grand Prix

Kawasaki KH125

In recent years, Kawasaki have diverted their attention from screaming untameable strokers to smooth, turbine-like four-stroke machines with even more performance. Bravely, in the light of pollution requirements, the company has persevered with two strokes and, even if the triples are but shadows of their past, they are still there.

The most recent addition to the two-stroke range is the KH125, a neat little commuter bike with a single-cylinder disc-valve engine of 124cc which produces 14.5bhp at 7500rpm. This, along with 10.5lb ft of torque, gives the 209lb bike a top speed of 73mph and enables it to cover a quarter mile from a standing start in 18.4secs. Fuel consumption is remarkably good for a stroker and averages out at 70mpg. Although not in the super economy four-stroke class, it is nevertheless good for a 125. The Kawasaki has a separate oil tank which makes things a whole lot easier when filling up: no more buying cans of oil and having nowhere to put them when you have taken out your mix!

The Kawasaki is a small bike, even for a 125, but this need not be a disadvantage. In fact, the sporting rider (or the rider with sporting pretentions) will find the semi-crouched position a boon in 'scratching' around town. In fact, the handling does fully live up to the style, and the little bike can be thrown around corners with gay abandon in complete safety. It feels taut and very responsive.

Braking is by means of a cable operated disc at the front and a drum at the rear, and the system is in keeping with the rest of the bike: efficient and trouble free.

However well the bike may corner and stop, it is the engine which is its most outstanding feature. It starts with the choke regularly on the first or second kick and, after a second or two, is willing to pull hard all the way up the rev range

through the six gears. For a two-stroke engine, it is very untemperamental and shows no tendency to foul up in traffic or misfire at slow speed. The disc valve helps make things smooth and efficient.

The KH125 comes complete with a rear view mirror (the twin mirrors of early bikes are now thought unnecessary), helmet lock, lockable seat with tool compartment in the tail fairing, steering lock and a very necessary tachometer. It may be a bit more expensive than most 125s, and may use more fuel than some, but in all it is a sophisticated and nimble bike and should prove very popular.

Engine
Air-cooled, single-cylinder two-stroke. 56mm (2.20in) bore × 50.6mm (1.99in) stroke = 124cc (7.56cu in). Maximum power (DIN) 14.5bhp at 7500rpm; maximum torque (DIN) 10.5lb ft at 6500rpm. Aluminium cylinder barrel and head. Compression ratio 7:1. 2 main bearings. 1 Mikuni carburettor.

Transmission
Multi-wet-plate clutch and six-speed gearbox. Ratios 1st 2.60, 2nd 1.69, 3rd 1.25, 4th 1.05, 5th 0.89, 6th 0.80:1. Chain drive to rear wheel.

Suspension
Telescopic fork front, and swinging arm with telescopic damper, rear.

Brakes
Disc front and drum rear.

Wheels and Tyres
2.75in × 18in front, 3.00in × 18in rear.

Weight
209lb (95kg).

Tank capacity
2.5gals (11.5 litres).

Seating
Dual saddle.

Performance
Maximum speed 73mph. Acceleration: standing start quarter mile 18.3secs. Fuel consumption approximately 70mpg.

Kawasaki Z650

Recently the 650cc capacity class has been resurrected. This once popular size of bike seemed to have died with Triumph and BSA, but the category has surged back with a Yamaha twin, and, in greater force, with the Z650 Kawasaki.

To the untrained eye, the Z650 looks exactly like its big brother, the famous Z1000. However, it is smaller in both looks and feel. The basis of the bike is a magnificent twin overhead camshaft, four-stroke, four-cylinder engine of 62mm × 54mm, giving a capacity of 652cc. With 64bhp produced at 8500rpm and a respectable 41.9lb ft of torque at 7000rpm, the Z650 is quick to say the least; that is but part of the story, however.

From quite low down the rev range, the bike pulls like a train and, when it comes on cam, it does not so much slam the rider in the back like earlier quick Kwackers, but just eases forward with great power and haste. This continues right into the red sector of the tachometer at 9000rpm when a quick snick of the delightfully light gearchange will start the whole thing happening again.

Top speed works out at a shade under 120mph while the standing start quarter mile time is a mite over thirteen seconds at 13.4. That is a brilliant performance for any machine let alone a 650. Because of the efficiency of the power unit, fuel consumption can be incredibly frugal and our average over the test was 48mpg. This included much hard riding but, with such an effortless engine, one just has to keep the right wrist firmly wound up on the throttle.

Whether one is brave enough to keep the power on for the corners is another matter. Big Kwackers have long had a reputation as bad handlers but the Z650 quickly gained respect as being docile. However, we found that if one was in two minds as to whether to power or coast through a bend the bike would respond by flexing and hopping on and off line. Should the rider brave it, things will be altogether more pleasing and it cheered us by cornering right over until the exhausts grounded.

Braking was something of a disappointment as the single front disc seemed unable to stop the machine continually from high speed without a great deal of fade; another disc at the front, for which there is provision, seems the obvious answer.

Wet weather braking of big Japanese bikes and their stainless steel discs is infamous, but the Z650 with its large rear drums tends to save the rider many heartaches.

Finish and equipment are both exemplary and a rider who wants trouble free riding and does not mind a few handling quirks will love the rather large middle-weight Kwacker. Of course, he will also get that rocket-like performance which is probably what Kawasaki riding is all about anyway.

Engine
Air-cooled, four-cylinder four-stroke. 62mm (2.44in) bore × 54mm (2.13in) stroke = 652cc (39.77cu in). Maximum power (DIN) 64bhp at 8500rpm; maximum torque (DIN) 41.9lb ft at 7000rpm. Aluminium cylinders and head. 2 valves per cylinder operated direct by twin overhead camshafts. Compression ratio 9.5:1. 5 main bearings.

Transmission
Multi-wet-plate clutch and five-speed gearbox. Ratios (not overall) 1st 15.626, 2nd 10.931, 3rd 8.517, 4th 6.975, 5th 5.569:1.

Suspension
Telescopic forks front and swinging arm with telescopic dampers rear.

Brakes
Disc front and drum rear.

Wheels and Tyres
3.25in × 19in front, 4in × 18in rear.

Weight
465lb (211kg).

Tank capacity
3.7gals (16.8litres).

Performance
Maximum speed 119mph. Acceleration: standing start quarter mile 13.4secs.

Kawasaki Z1000

The Z1000 Kawasaki is the successor to the legendary 900 Z bikes which have long reigned supreme as everybody's ideal of ultimate road performance on two wheels.

There were many myths about the 'King Kwacker' and many would swear that it could out accelerate a Formula One racing car up to about 100mph. In reality, that was something of an exaggeration but it was very quick. As it grew older, emission regulations knocked a bhp or two off here and there until the makers decided to reinstate the performance by

making the bike a nice round thousand; in fact, this was turning the full circle as the big Z prototypes tested initially in America were of 1 litre capacity.

The change from 903cc to the present 1015cc has made the Z1000 a lot more docile and, although the bhp figure has not gone up a great deal, the torque curve is a little flatter. Top speed of the bike is 125mph while the standing start quarter mile time is a mere 12.3secs. Fuel consumption averages out at 40mpg.

Getting all the performance out of the bike is not the easiest of tasks. Firstly, the twist grip has far too much movement and needs almost 'two handfuls' to get it round to the stop. Although this is annoying when pulling away from rest, it can be a nuisance and disconcerting when changing gear: as one eases off the throttle from maximum twist and releases the clutch, there is still enough throttle opening to send the revs soaring over the red line. Secondly, the high-rise bars make upper speed range performance very tiring and a

nice big fairing would make a wonderful addition.

That aside, one cannot fail to be impressed by such a remarkable power unit. It is smooth, quiet and economical in the lower rev range but, when given the reins, it is transformed into a screaming force which will rocket the 540lb machine along at an alarming rate. The power does not come in all of a sudden, it is there all the time right through the range.

With the high bars and the rider's upright position, the machine seems very large and

Kawasaki Z1000

one feels not so much in command of the bike as *vice versa*. Go too fast and it will feel as if it has a hinge in the middle; ease off the throttle in corners, however, and it will be smooth and trouble free. Twin discs at the front and a single disc at the rear make stopping an incident free affair.

It has been said that the Z1000 is *the* 'untameable road machine'. Try to gentle it and you may regret it, but live with it and exploit it from time to time and you should be an extremely satisfied biker.

Engine
Air-cooled, four-cylinder four-stroke. 70mm (2.75in) bore × 66mm (2.59in) stroke = 1015cc (61.93cu in). Maximum power (DIN) 83bhp at 8000rpm; maximum torque (DIN) 58.7lb ft at 6500rpm. Aluminium cylinders and head. 2 valves per cylinder operated direct by twin overhead camshafts. Compression ratio 8.7:1. 5 main bearings. 4 Mikuni carburettors.

Transmission
Multi-wet-plate clutch and five-speed gearbox. Ratios (overall) 1st 12.1, 2nd 8.34, 3rd 6.35, 4th 5.26, 5th 4.64:1. Chain drive to rear wheel.

Suspension
Telescopic forks front and swinging arm with telescopic dampers rear.

Brakes
Double discs front and single disc rear.

Wheels and Tyres
3.25in × 19in front, 4in × 18in rear.

Weight
540lb (245kg).

Tank capacity
3.7gals (16.8 litres).

Seating
Dual saddle.

Performance
Maximum speed 125mph. Acceleration: standing start quarter mile 12.3secs. Fuel consumption 40mpg.

Above: not to be outdone by rivals Honda with their CBX, Kawasaki upped the capacity of their six when the large Honda was announced. This is the Z1300 water-cooled, shaft-drive monster

Above right: the neat Custom 650

Below: sports version of the famous Z1000 is the Z-1R

Right: although most Kawasakis were designed for the US market, they built some specifically for Britain, too. This is the four-stroke twin, the Z250

Getting it Going

THE KICKSTARTER (or kickstart, if you prefer) appeared around 1911 and became a feature of virtually all road-going motor cycles until quite recently when electric starting began seriously to penetrate the market. Before the kickstarting era, various means were used to get the engine going: on machines with pedals, the rider had to twirl these with the machine either on or off the stand; others (such as the 1906 Denell) had a car-type starting handle engaging the end of the crankshaft; yet others were started by pushing or by putting them on the stand and tweaking the rear wheel.

Obscure as are its precise origins, the kickstarter certainly became practicable as soon as clutches and transmission systems with a neutral position came into use. In essence, it is a pedal-operated mechanism which rotates the engine through the engaged clutch (with the gearbox in neutral) and commonly, therefore, through the primary drive as well.

Although a number of layouts were tried in earlier days, two principal types soon became established. Both had, of course, to incorporate a ratchet-and-pawl or freewheel arrangement to allow the pedal to return – under spring-loading – after each stroke, ready for the next prod.

In one of these types, the free-return device was coaxial with the pedal spindle while, in the other, it was on a gear which was engaged by a toothed quadrant or sector mounted on the spindle. Consideration of directions of rotation shows that, with a chain primary drive, the first system had to operate on the gearbox layshaft while the second had to rotate the mainshaft. For the layshaft scheme to work, too, the two gearbox shafts had to be coupled by a pair of gears constantly in mesh.

Sunbeam were among the earliest makers to fit a kickstarter, which featured on their first models two years or so before World War I. They chose the quadrant layout but, because

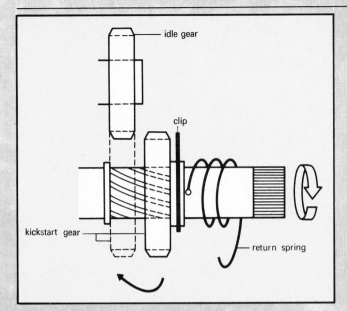

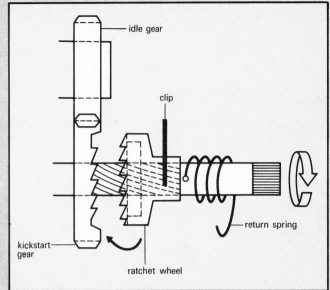

their motor cycles had 'crossover' drive (with the primary chain on the left and the rear chain on the right), the pinion had to be inserted on the mainshaft between the clutch and the gearbox. Consequently, a cross-shaft was mounted behind the gearbox, carrying the quadrant at the left-hand end and the pedal at the other, for actuation by the normally stronger right leg. When both drives were on the left of the engine, the design could obviously be simplified since the kickstarter could then drive directly on to the end of the appropriate gearbox shaft.

In the forms described so far, both the mainshaft and layshaft kickstarters are suitable for any machines with transverse crankshafts, and both designs are still used today. What happens, however, when the crankshaft is longitudinal? In the case of BMW, the answer is nothing: the German company's flat-twins (and the singles it used to make) merely had the pedal on a longitudinal spindle, moving in a transverse arc instead of a fore-and-aft one. As a result, only a contortionist could start one while on the machine; he had to place himself beside it, preferably with it on the stand. Perhaps BMW were guilty of plagiarism, since the transverse-twin ABC of immediately after World War I had a similar system.

Another German maker, Zündapp, built big flat-twins with transverse cylinders for some years from the late 1930s. They were a bit more clever than BMW and ABC, in that they inserted a 90° bevel drive in the kickstarter mechanism, thus bringing the pedal arc into the conventional and more convenient plane. Right-angle gearing was employed also in several British post-war motor cycles with longitudinal crankshafts – the in-line Sunbeam S7/S8, the transverse-twin Velocettes (LE and Valiant) and Douglas models. The Sunbeams, Douglases and Valiant had orthodox kickstarters but the LE (in keeping with its genteel appearance, and thanks to its small cylinders) had a hand lever to bring the engine to life.

Yet another variation on the longitudinal-crankshaft theme had appeared in 1931 – from AJS on the big transverse veetwin of which one or two examples are still around. This machine had a 90° bevel drive between the flywheel clutch and the gearbox which therefore had transverse shafts and so presented no problems with the kickstarter. Do not think, however, that the latter was the reason for 'bending' the drive in this way: the 'Ajay' had chain final drive, not the shaft that one would have expected.

A kickstarter has to be correctly geared in relation to the cylinder size and the compression ratio of the engine. Gear it too high and only the heavyweight rider will be able to bounce the engine over compression; gear it too low, on the other hand, and it will not spin the crankshaft effectively. The gearing

depends partly on the ratio of the primary drive, if any, and partly on the relative sizes of the quadrant and its pinion, or on the ratio of the constant-mesh gears, as appropriate.

Our final variable here is of course the length of the pedal crank which affects the mechanical advantage and therefore the effort needed. However, only a limited amount of lengthening is practicable if the resistance is found to be unduly high, owing to the physical difficulty of operating a very long pedal and the latter's obtrusive nature when not in use. AB

Above left: a non-constant-mesh system; when the pedal is kicked the inertia of the starter gear drives it along the Bendix screw and into mesh with the idler gear

Above: a constant-mesh system; the ratchet wheel is driven into engagement with the start gear when the pedal is kicked

Far left: pedals for starting on a pre-kickstart Pope

Below: the kickstart shaft on a Suzuki GT750 three-cylinder, two-stroke machine

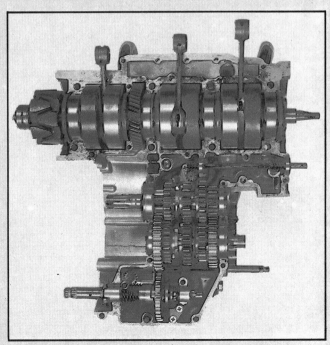

The Showman Superb

promising athlete and hockey player, the stunt rider bug had already bitten deep.

When he was only nine years old, Knievel saw auto daredevil Joey Chitwood use a take-off ramp to leapfrog his car over another vehicle. Bob went straight home and took down his grandfather's garage doors to make a jumping ramp for his bicycle. With the help of his younger brother, who was himself to become involved in motor sport later on, Bob put on a show for the neighbourhood kids which climaxed in a jump through blazing brushwood and, thanks to the enthusiasm of his brother stoking the fire, blazing garage doors as well.

Young Knievel's first venture onto a powered two-wheeler was equally fraught with disaster. His father got him a small motor cycle which he promptly ran into a mailbox at the end of his street. In time his skill with motor cycles grew, and after several short-lived attempts to start careers in such widely varied fields as insurance salesman, pole vaulter, hunter's guide, rodeo cowboy, even as a small-time safe-breaker, he found his true vocation as a motor cycle stunt rider.

In his early teens, Knievel was a keen competitor on local racetracks. So keen in fact, that 'they would start me in the back row, facing the opposite direction, and I'd still win'. The sport offered little financial reward however, so he approached potential sponsors with the idea of a motor cycle stunt show run along the lines of the car shows that had inspired him as a lad. The scheme sounded promising; Norton came forward with the machinery, and Evel Knievel's Motorcycle Daredevils were on the road.

The exact origin of the name 'Evel' is, like so much of the folklore surrounding Knievel, a little hazy. Certainly, there would appear to be some truth in the story that, as a teenager, Knievel once found himself in Butte's town jail alongside a local villain by the name of 'Awful' Knofol. Stealing hubcaps was a national pastime amongst young Americans, and with his typical verve Knievel had amassed over three hundred of them before the police finally caught up with him. He claimed to have bought them from a tramp – he even produced a receipt signed 'Hobo Joe' which had the police station in uproar – and while the neighbourhood hubcap syndicate was being brought to task, and parents were sent for, the word got out that they had 'Awful' Knofol and 'Evil' Knievel in the jail.

Knievel claims that the nickname went back still further to his junior school days where a baseball umpire

Robert Craig Knievel, better known to the world as 'Evel' Knievel, is probably the greatest motor cycle stunt rider of all times. He has jumped further and higher, over more varied objects than anyone else. He has broken so many bones that even he has now lost count. One leg has a steel support, surgically implanted, which measures three inches by two feet; other bits of metal connect other parts of his interior at various points. In 1973 he made over a million dollars jumping motor cycles over cars and trucks; the following year he earned an incredible six million dollars for an attempt to cross the Snake River Canyon, Idaho, in his jet-propelled 'Skycycle'.

Daredevil, poet, orator, showman, madman; whatever guise Knievel chose he could not be ignored. His loyalties are true blue American; his view of women is blatantly chauvinistic; he loves motor cycles and motor cycle sport but condemns the 'black leather jacket' image. He is outspoken about his prowess as a rider, his loathing of narcotics and his belief that 'might is right'. He is on record as saying, 'God created all men, and Winchester made 'em equal, and that's just the way I think'. He has been variously described as 'a born loser who doesn't know it', 'the Muhammad Ali of wheels' and the 'American Medical Association's Man of the Year'. He sees himself as an explorer, a pioneer in the art of stunt driving and motor cycling, the 'Last Gladiator of the New Rome'.

Born in Butte, Montana, on 15 October 1939, Knievel inherited his love for high speed thrills from his father who raced midgets and sports cars. His parents were divorced when he was very young and he went to live with his grandparents who were to see him through school and later send him to hockey school, University of North Dakota. Although he shaped-up as a

Previous page: Harley-Davidson star Knievel in a sea of bikes explains to a young fan the technique of jumping

This page: the Skycycle on its launching ramp prior to Evel's most famous stunt of all

gave him the tag because of the looks he gave the opposition on the pitch. Knievel changed the spelling 'because it it was an unnecessary evil'.

Evel Knievel's early stunt programmes included doing 'wheelies' – riding his machines at speed with the front wheel held high in the air – and crashing through walls of fire. His first public jump was at a race track at Moses Lake, Washington, where his stunt team were to provide the half-time entertainment. The obstacle consisted of a pair of tethered mountain lions and a hundred live rattlesnakes in boxes. Evel wickedly relates how he clipped one of the boxes on landing and the snakes got out and made for the audience. 'People were running every which way. It was a real crowd pleaser, you might say!'

Those first few years were hard going; Evel was the team's manager, promoter and star attraction, and when he got hurt the others just had to sit around

Left: Evel Knievel warming up for another spectacular motor cycle jump. Knievel's machine is a mighty Harley-Davidson. Knievel is perhaps the best known of all stunt jumpers and his achievements have resulted in the activity now being recognised as a proper sport. Indeed, Knievel, by 1977, was one of the world's highest paid sportsmen

Below: Evel Knievel prepares himself for a jump at the British Wembley Stadium in May 1975. His target was to clear thirteen single decker buses. Unfortunately Knievel's landing on the boarded ramp was mistimed and he crashed heavily, breaking his pelvis once again

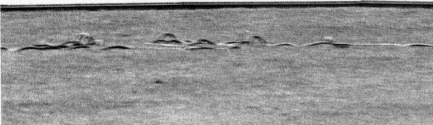

and wait till he got better. Regular crashes and regular lay-offs were all part of the game, but Evel Knievel kept coming back for more. Once, in Oklahoma City, he jumped three cars with a broken back and his body in a cast. The press were unsympathetic – they said he should have waited until he could have made a more spectacular display, but for Knievel the show had to go on. The promoter had laid out 10,000 dollars, the fans were expecting him, the challenge could not be resisted.

Between 1966 and 1971 Evel Knievel underwent nine major operations as a result of eleven crashes out of a total of almost two hundred jumps. By 1977 he was never without his gold-topped walking cane, seemingly, at first glance just part of his striking outfit – an all-white suit criss-crossed with star spangled stripes, and flowing cape. Then one noticed his pronounced limp – a grim reminder of his worst accident which happened at Caesar's Palace, Las Vegas.

In front of 20,000 spectators, Knievel jumped the geyser-like fountains outside the famous casino, only to come down slightly sideways on the landing ramp. The Triumph motor cycle was unable to withstand the shock of the impact, the rear wheel collapsed and Evel catapulted over the handlebars to slam, bounce and somersault for fifty yards across the asphalt arena. In hospital, recovering from fractures of the hip, pelvis and ribs, he vowed never to jump over asphalt again and set about planning his next stunt.

They billed his appearance at the Pocono Raceway as the last motor cycle performance of the year in Pocono; it was almost the last performance, anywhere, motor cycle or not, for Evel Knievel. Things had not been going too well for him and his previous two jumps had resulted in minor spills. Undaunted, he went through his by now familiar pre-jump routine of high speed runs and wheelies, warming up the bike and setting the crowd on the edge of their seats. Then, he blasted up the take-off ramp and into the air . . . and silence. His engine had stalled, the bike crossed-up, and once more he was flung down the landing ramp like a rag doll. He suffered a broken sternum, broken right hand, three broken ribs and a broken shoulder. Helped to his feet, he walked to the commentators box on the start/finish line and apologised to the audience.

1970 witnessed two of Knievel's most spectacular, and most successful jumps. In February of that year, before a crowd of 70,000, he made an assault on the world record for motor cycle jumps over automobiles. Nineteen cars were lined-up side-by-side across the infield at California's Ontario Motor Speedway, the last five tucked beneath the landing ramp lest he should fall short of the target. The precaution was unnecessary; riding a powerful Harley-Davidson XR-750, the American factory's purpose-built flat-track racer, he cleared the jump with graceful ease, covering a total in-air distance of forty-three yards and establishing a new world record.

Above and right: one of Knievel's most publicised but least successful stunts was his attempt to jump the Snake River Canyon on his rocket-powered Skycycle. On the jump, however, a parachute opened too early, causing the machine to crash into the canyon

Two months later, in Seattle, he went for eighteen cars with a preliminary warm-up over thirteen. The first jump almost ended in disaster when the bike's rear wheel caught the lip of the landing ramp, slamming the front of the machine down hard just as it had in Las Vegas. But this time Evel was able to hang on and bring the bike to a controlled halt. The wet grass of the race circuit's infield had robbed the machine of traction and the necessary power for take-off. Reluctantly, Knievel watched as the eighteen-car jump was set up on the Seattle Raceway's asphalt track, although his worries were short-lived. With the essential grip restored to the bike's rear wheel his second jump went perfectly and Evel Knievel confirmed his title as 'King of Stuntmen'.

With a world record to his credit, and an extremely healthy bank balance for his efforts, Evel Knievel could have sat back in the luxury of his new home in Butte, Montana, enjoyed the company of his wife, Linda, and their three children, played all the golf he wanted – his second passion to motor cycles – and waited for somebody to come up with a challenge.

As far back as 1966 Evel Knievel announced that he was to perform the ultimate motor cycle stunt – to jump the Grand Canyon. In fact, permission was granted by America's Department of the Interior for the jump to take place, but the project ran into opposition from the Navaho Indians and the location was finally switched to Snake River Canyon in Idaho. Evel bought 300 acres of the Canyon and

drew about him a team of promoters and designers the like of which the stunt world had never seen before.

While film, television and book rights were arranged, rocket expert Robert Truax set about designing and building a suitable vehicle. Obviously, a conventional motor cycle was out of the question, the distance from one side to the other at the chosen point, Twin Falls, being just short of a mile. His solution was a vehicle similar in appearance to land speed record machines used at Bonneville Salt Flats, a two-wheeled projectile seventeen feet long and twenty-five inches in diameter, powered by steam rocket.

The vehicle was named the 'Skycycle' and a prototype, the X-1, was test-fired over the Canyon in November 1973. It failed miserably, and so a more powerful model X-2 was built and the angle of the launch ramp was increased from 22 degrees to 56. The X-2 performed the launching procedure perfectly, but the small drogue chute which was supposed to pull out the main parachute after the apogee of some 3000 feet was reached above the centre of the Canyon, malfunctioned. It opened too early, causing the X-2 to plunge at full speed into the river below.

Unfortunately for Knievel, on 8 September 1974 – the date of his most spectacular jump attempt ever – a similar malfunction caused the drogue chute to open even before the 'Skycycle' X-3 had cleared the launch ramp, and a crowd of 40,000 spectators, with another estimated 1½ million gathered in cinemas throughout the United States to watch on closed circuit TV, stood

horrified as it drifted down into the gorge, bumping the lava rock walls as it went.

Evel received only minor cuts and bruises and the attempt netted him an incredible six million dollar purse, but it had failed. For many the stunt had been too outrageous to be anything more than an elaborate con trick, and Knievel's credibility suffered accordingly.

Evel didn't jump again until 26 May 1975, when he appeared at Wembley Stadium, London, England; his target, thirteen single-decker buses, side-by-side. The crowd were sceptical, they had come to see him jump, not to hear him sing the praises of Mother America and revile the misuse of narcotics by her youth, and they were noticeably restless until they heard the roar of his Harley. He swooped from a sky-type approach slope high in the grandstand, cleared the buses, then crashed painfully onto the boarded off-ramp.

His pelvis smashed once more, Evel Knievel insisted on returning to the top of the ramp to address the crowd. 'I will never jump again,' he told them. Even if his words should prove true, nobody could honestly say that he was finally beaten. As he once said himself, 'It is better for a person to take a chance from life . . . than to live in that grey twilight and know not victory nor defeat'.   PM

Below: not quite what it seems. In his film Viva Knievel, Evel had a stunt man to stand in for him. Here, Gary Davis jumps the Knievel Harley-Davidson 120 feet over a cage of wild cats

King of the midgets

While other makes may rightly claim greater impact on 50cc road racing at international level over a short period than may Kreidler – Honda for instance, Suzuki certainly and Derbi perhaps – for sustained effort and high performance over several years, few would doubt the claims of the little Kreidler company.

This West German factory, which concentrates on the manufacture of 50cc mopeds and lightweight motor cycles, was set up in 1950 and built its reputation with a 50cc Grand Prix racing machine which contested the first 50cc world championship in 1962. To Kreidler goes the distinction of winning the first-ever 50cc world championship event in the modern series, the Spanish GP at Barcelona, when Hans-Georg Anscheidt took them to victory against Honda and Derbi. Good performances during the year by Anscheidt and Dutch rider Busquet, saw Kreidler faring well in 1962 and these two riders finished the season in second and fourth places in that first 50cc championship.

In the class Suzuki were supreme, but although Suzuki took the title for the second year running, Anscheidt on the Kreidler ran close, and with wins in Spain, France and Finland, was only three points short of the title after the ninth and final round. The competition had become keener and Hugh Anderson claimed the title for Suzuki after a season-long battle.

Facing intense rivalry from Suzuki and Honda, who during 1964 produced a 50cc twin which could be raced at over 100mph, Kreidler continued the battle, though with much less resources than the major Japanese factories. For the third year running, Anscheidt took the Spanish GP title though he lost ground in the championship, finishing third to Anderson on the Suzuki and Ralph Bryan's Honda.

Not surprisingly, the West German factory was beginning to wilt under the Japanese onslaught in the class and midway through 1965, cut down their factory support. In October that year – shortly after the withdrawal of Derbi – the Kreidler factory announced their decision not to enter works riders and machines in 50cc races in 1966. The powerhouse challenge of Japan, in the form of Honda and Suzuki, was now left on its own to fight for the title. After battling unsuccessfully on the Kreidler, Anscheidt switched to Suzuki after the West German factory's withdrawal, and gained a well-earned world title for the first time in 1966 over Ralph Bryans on the works Honda racer.

Those early Kreidler race machines were equipped with fourteen gears and it says much for Anscheidt's skill that he eventually succeeded in mastering the machine and was able to finish runner-up in the world championship of 1962 and '63.

That might have ended the Kreidler racing story, but after an absence of three years, Kreidlers were once again seen on the Grand Prix circuits, mainly due to a new ruling from the FIM and through the initiative of Dutch importer Van Veen, who financed a team of racing machines himself.

The crippling costs of Grand Prix success at such an exotic level, as developed by the Japanese factories, had in the end led to them pulling out of the sport and the FIM restricted the number of cylinders and gear ratios in the hope of

Overleaf: Hans-Georg Anscheidt, winner of the 1961 Coupe d'Europe event at Zandvoort, on his 50cc Kreidler

Left: close up of the tiny 50cc engine used in the 1973 Van Veen Kreidler Grand Prix racer

Below: a view of Kreidler's factory in West Germany

Bottom: Henk van Kessel used a Kreidler to become the 1974 50cc World Champion

Opposite page, top: the 50cc Kreidler Florett Super TS of 1967

Opposite page, below: Rudolf Kunz's Kreidler record breaker at Utah in 1965

encouraging smaller manufacturers back into racing. Honda's retirement, after contesting the 1966 50cc championship with a double overhead camshaft twin and a ten-speed gearbox, had left only Suzuki's two-stroke twin with twelve or fourteen speed gearboxes in the field; and they too were to depart leaving only Anscheidt to win the 1968 title on the Suzuki before the restrictions were imposed.

Originally the new rulings were intended for 1970, but with the class starved after such exciting years of works involvement, the FIM advanced their legislation by a year. The move brought back Kreidler, along with Derbi and the small Dutch Jamathi factory, into the 50cc class in 1969.

Van Veen fielded Aalt Toersen and former Dutch 50cc champion Jan de Vries and both did well in the early rounds with first and third for Toersen and de Vries in Spain, and a first and second in the same order in Germany. Toersen made it three consecutive wins with victory in France, but in later rounds was eased out by the Derbi machines of Smith and Herrero. Even so, Toersen led the 50cc world championship table on the Kreidler until the final round. Angel Nieto on the Spanish made Derbi finally took the title.

Dutch importer Van Veen had started to develop his own Kreidlers in 1964

when the factory quit racing, and the 1969 machines embodied much of the manufacturer's technical know-how. Developed from the production road models, the frame of the Van Veen racers was identical with that of the last factory 12-speed racers of five years before. The air-cooled engine had a rotary-disc inlet valve, and power output was about 15.5bhp at 14,500rpm; but the effective power band was over only a very narrow 1000rpm.

After leaving racing, the Kreidler factory displayed renewed interest once Aalt Toersen had set world records in Britain in October 1968.

The machines made little impact in 1970, but in 1971, with new riders Jan de Vries and Rudolf Kunz, they carried the attack into the Derbi and Jamathi camps and with outright wins in Austria, Germany, Belgium, Italy and Spain, De Vries brought Kreidler their first world title. Two other Kreidlers were produced to give some back-up to the main pair and these were ridden, interestingly enough, by the British racer Barry Sheene and the Finnish star who was to become a world champion the very next year, Jarno Saarinen. In the 50cc championship of 1971, Sheene won the Czechoslovakian GP at Brno, but Saarinen's best placing was in the last round in Spain, where he finished second, Kreidler machines taking four of the top six places.

Kreidler and Derbi machines fought for the honours in 1972 with Jamathi somewhat out of contention. It was a battle between De Vries and Nieto and at the end of an exciting season, De Vries had taken the Kreidler to three wins, level with Nieto on the Derbi. They each had three second places to their credit. Both had 69 points, but Nieto sneaked the title for Derbi by 21 seconds, after the times in the five races in which both were placed were added together and compared.

The withdrawal of Derbi from racing shortly after, left the way clear for the Van Veen Kreidler machines. De Vries took the title in 1973 for a second time, his last season before retirement. Kreidler, through Bruno Kneubuhler, took second place, with fourth and fifth gained by Thurow and Van Kessel.

From 1973 to 1975, Kreidler dominated 50cc racing. After De Vries' retirement, Henk van Kessel took up the challenge, taking the title in 1974. His machine was not a works Van Veen, but a stock racing Kreidler equipped with a standard racing Van Veen kit. The Dutch company had developed the already fast Kreidlers into machines of much improved efficiency, and in 1973 Van Kessel realised that without good machinery he could not hope to secure the championship. Four Van Veen Kreidlers were up for sale at around £4000 each. An enthusiastic fan club helped out and was said to have hired the use of one of the racing machines on a meeting-by-meeting basis.

Kreidler machines now dominated the 50cc scene and development was so intense in the class that lap records were tumbling at many circuits. Thanks to the FIMs six-speed gearbox limitation, however, engine tuning was directed along the right lines of broad power. Kessel's machine produced its most effective power (21bhp at the crankshaft) at 14,000rpm and continued up to 17,000, a band which equalled that of the 125s and 250s.

In 1974 the twenty-eight-year-old Van Kessel romped through the championship rounds, competing in ten races and winning six to gain maximum points. At Francorchamps, the Van Veen Kreidler was timed at 125.5mph along the fastest straight, and raised the lap record to 101.07mph, against the previous record of 100.74mph set by Jan de Vries, also on a Kreidler. That year Kreidler machines occupied all top five places in the 50cc world championship table, a remarkable achievement for such a small factory.

Angel Nieto had bought one of the ex-factory Van Veens and with his rival from previous years, De Vries, as tuner, took the title in 1975 with considerable ease. In the close season, however, Nieto persuaded Bultaco, for whom he had

Top: the lovely Kreidler Florett 'Elektronik' model of 1977 may only have a 50cc engine, but it is a perfect mini lightweight motor cycle in anyone's language

Above centre: engine of the 1977 Kreidler Cross two-stroke enduro machine

Right: Kreidler works rider Aalt Toersen took this tiny record breaker to Britain in 1968 and used it to establish a number of new speed records. Much of Kreidler's history has been taken up by its record breaking sporting attempts both in Europe and the United States of America

ridden some years before, to provide a specially tuned machine for the championship, and this move probably prevented what would have been another world title for Kreidler.

As it was, the Kreidlers of Herbert Rittberger and Ulrich Graf were second and third in the final table and in the top 26 placings Kreidler machines occupied no fewer than eighteen positions, with Kreidler hybrids like the ABF and Theo Timmer's Jamathi/Kreidler giving the name three more placings. It was a magnificent display of in-depth domination.

Apart from Grand Prix racing, Kreidler have had occasional ambitions in speed record attempts. In 1965 Rudolf Kunz set new world records for the flying kilometre and mile at the Utah Salt Flats in the United States, when a specially supercharged, streamlined machine reached an incredible one-way speed of 140.02mph and averaged 130.88mph for the 'there and back' kilometre runs and 130.00mph for the mile record.

Preparations for these attempts had been started two years before when the Kreidler factory consulted Vaifro Meo (holder of a number of world records in the early 'fifties) about the design and layout of a possible record-breaking machine. Then Kreidler began constructing two machines of almost identical layout. The engines followed closely the lines of the single-cylinder, two-stroke Kreidler racers, but had superchargers fitted to both engines to improve efficiency and counteract the reduced atmospheric pressure at the Salt Flats. The machines were wind tunnel tested in Stuttgart and later raced round the Hockenheim circuit.

The new records broke those set nine years before when West German H. P. Muller clocked 121.70mph for both distances in the famous two-stroke-powered NSU, and the 140.02mph (225km/h) was an absolute world record for 50cc engines.

Domestically, the Kreidler machine has breeding, maintains high engineering standards and places much emphasis on reliability and long life. In fact the company has a golden pin and plaque award scheme for Kreidler owners on completion of 100,000km. The Florett Sports has been a popular model and was based on the West German factory's regular 50cc roadsters with a horizontal single-cylinder two-stroke engine and a top speed of over 45mph.

The manufacturers category of the world championship has been won consistently by Kreidler since 1971 up to 1976, when they yielded the title to Bultaco by a single point and, although Bultaco also took the riders world title through Nieto, Kreidler machines occupied nine of the first twelve places. PC

Van Veen OCR 1000

Most of Henk van Veen's involvement with motor cycles has revolved around the tiny 50cc racers produced by the Kreidler factory, for whom Van Veen is the Dutch agent. So when it came to building his own bikes, it came as a complete surprise when Van Veen launched the incredible OCR 1000.

The OCR 1000 was intended by Van Veen to be the ultimate superbike, a high-quality, luxury, high-speed, limited-production machine aimed at a specific, and very wealthy, market. And you need to be wealthy to afford the OCR because £5500 was the estimated asking price in Britain by mid 1977.

What exactly makes the OCR 1000 so expensive? For a start it is no ordinary machine. The whole bike is totally hand-built and the engine is a two-rotor Wankel-type motor of 996cc, developed in conjunction with the Audi/NSU company in Germany, and reputed to produce a staggering 100bhp. This gives the 650lb monster an estimated top speed of 150mph.

The frame of the big OCR 1000 was designed by Jaap Voskamp who also designed the Kreidler racing bike frames. Both the front forks and the rear suspension are by Koni, while the gearbox and shaft drive were developed at the Porsche car factory in Stuttgart.

To stop the big beast, twin Brembo disc brakes are fitted at the front while a single disc is used at the rear.

No motor cycling journalist in Britain has been able to lay his hands on an OCR 1000 for long enough to be able to put it through a comprehensive road test, but two points have been raised by brief road impressions.

One is that the 150mph top speed is probably an exaggeration, but not by much, while the other point is that the rotary engine has a big thirst. Even with a $4\frac{3}{4}$ gallon fuel tank, this makes long distance touring a tricky proposition.

But perhaps the only way to find out properly would be to lay £5500 at Henk van Veen's feet and ask him to build you one.

Engine

Water cooled, twin rotor Wankel type. $2 \times 498cc = 996cc$ (60.75cu in). Maximum power

100bhp at 6000rpm. One Solex DDITS carburettor with twin 32mm chokes.

Transmission
Hydraulically-operated multi-plate clutch. Four-speed gearbox with left foot change. Ratios 1st 2.35, 2nd 1.61, 3rd 1.1, 4th 0.88.

Suspension
Front – damped telescopic, rear – damped swinging arm.

Brakes
Twin discs front, single disc rear.

Wheels and Tyres
4.25 × 18in front and rear. Tyres 110/90 V18 Pirelli front, 120/90 V18 Pirelli rear.

Weight
650lb (295kg).

Tank capacity
4.75 gallons.

Seating
Dual seat.

Performance
Maximum speed around 150mph. Fuel consumption approximately 30mpg.

Over the years history has brought together a number of famous two-somes; partnerships of people who managed to exist quite comfortably on their own but who, until fate brought them into contact with a person whose talents complemented theirs, failed to achieve the real success that they were capable of. Such a twosome were Kronreif and Trunkenpolz who met in Mattighofen, Austria, and whose initials and that of the place where they met go together to form the name KTM.

It is a common misconception that motor cycle production at Mattighofen began just after World War II in 1947 or 1948. In fact, motor cycles first started to roll out of the Austrian factory in 1951 and previous to that it had existed as an engineering workshop for seventeen years, being set up by Herr Trunkenpolz in 1934. Throughout the years the company's machines have been powered by a variety of other manufacturers' engines, including Rotax, Sachs and Puch – the other of Austria's two motor cycle makers. Rotax's connections with the company date back to the very beginning, for the first bike produced by Trunkenpolz's firm, the R100, was powered by one of their 100cc two-stroke power units. Although never a great success – only 1000 machines were sold in the first year – this first effort at least did well enough to maintain Herr Trunkenpolz's interest and encouraged him to commit further capital investment for the development of new models.

Not only did Trunkenpolz start to plough money into the development of new road going machinery but, wisely deciding that success in competition was the best publicity for an up and coming motor cycle maker, he also concentrated part of his efforts into the fields of time trials and road racing. Factory teams were formed and the 125cc class – only given recognition by the FIM at the start of the 1950s – was settled upon as the arena for the company to make their big breakthrough into road race competition.

Great attention was paid to detail on the new road race bikes and they could not have had a better engine than the re-designed MV Agusta 125cc ohc four-stroke, single-cylinder motor with which they were fitted. Although KTM achieved a modicum of success, the new ultra-lightweight class proved to be a benefit for the Italian firms Mondial and MV

Below: the KTM name is one of the most respected in motocross. Here is one of their 250cc single-cylinder two-stroke models in action

Joining forces

Agusta and the Austrian bikes were eventually withdrawn. Nevertheless, hard work and perseverance over the years were to bring KTM their just rewards and had he lived no one would have been more pleased than Herr Trunkenpolz to see the company that he founded lift the 250cc World Motocross Championship in 1974.

The progression of events in the development of KTM's road going machinery is the exact reverse of that of most motor cycle makers. Whereas the majority of other manufacturers seem to have started with the construction of bicycles, from whence they progressed to the clipping of small auxiliary motors to their bicycle frames and from there to the production of motor cycles proper, in the case of KTM, as we have seen, motor cycle production came first. It was not until 1953 that the company added mopeds to their range and not until another nine years had passed that they made a complete return to grass roots with an entry into the field of bicycle manufacture.

Instead of testing the water first, in 1953 the factory went straight into the deep end of moped production and released a range of five models. Powered by a variety of two-stroke engines ranging from 50 to 125cc these models consisted of the Mecky, Tourist 125, Mirabell-Roller, Tarzan and Mustang. Of these the sporty looking Mustang proved to be the most successful and, with its rugged-

Above: André Malherbe in action on his KTM during the 1976 Dutch 250cc Motocross Grand Prix event

Right: the 1970 50cc Comet Super 4 model

factory had been increased beyond all recognition.

The partnership ended in 1960, with the untimely death of Herr Kronreif, but by then plans for new models were well in advance and the strategy that KTM were to follow throughout the difficult years of the 1960s was already laid down. Coinciding with the death of Kronreif, the running of design and development at Mattighofen fell to an engineer named Zizala. It was he who brought a fresh approach to much of KTM's design work and to him goes much of the credit for the development the motor cycles and mopeds that were produced by the factory throughout the 1960s and into the 1970s.

Left: the single-cylinder, two-stroke engine of the 250cc KTM motocross machine of 1975

Below: the highly competitive 1974 KTM 400MC scrambler

Bottom: works rider Willi Bauer and the 400cc 1977 KTM Grand Prix machine

The year 1962 brought about the end of an era at KTM and a change in the company's structure. Three major factors contributed to this change, the most important of these being that Herr Trunkenpolz died and his son Erich took control of the firm. Also in that year, as already stated, bicycle production started and the first of what was to become a comprehensive range of pedal powered vehicles left the factory. Added to these two happenings, KTM decided that the scooter boom of the early 1960s was too good an opportunity to ignore. They entered this competitive sector with the Ponny-Roller, a scooter which caught for the company a healthy share of the market and which remained in production in an almost unchanged state right through to 1977.

Showing the cordiality which seems to exist between KTM and their Austrian neighbours Puch, the Ponny and its more lavishly fitted sister scooter the Ponny L were powered by a Puch single-cylinder, 50cc, two-stroke engine with a fan cooling system. Unlike the majority of other

ness and reliability, so impressed the Army that it led to the company capturing a large contract from the Austrian Armed Forces. This put the factory on a sound footing and as time progressed moped production was to form the cornerstone of KTM's success.

A firm foundation may have been achieved but that certain sparkle that was to lead to a boom in the fortunes of KTM was still missing. The ingredient that was missing arrived in 1954 and came in the form of Kronreif, a man of considerable engineering skill and business acumen. Taking an interest in the firm he became a partner and his talents, added to those of Trunkenpolz, spelt success for the Mattighofen motor cycle concern. The two men blended together perfectly and within a short time production at the

scooters the four-speed gearbox was operated by a foot change system and again, unlike its contemporaries, the kick start was situated not under the running board but halfway up the side of the bike, a system which called for a certain degree of agility from its rider. The Ponny L was extremely well equipped with standard accessories including lockable luggage compartment, tachometer, electric indicators, a luggage carrier and rubber floor mats. Excellent value for money and a design ahead of its time were the main contributing factors to the Ponny's success. The appearance of the bike even well into the 1970s did not look outdated.

The 1960s proved to be very lean years for a lot of central European motor cycle makers. Only the Japanese seemed to be able to find a ready market for their machines. So KTM in common with many of their European counterparts pulled in their horns and concentrated on the manufacture and development of mopeds, scooters and bicycles. Lean years for motor cycle makers they may have been but they led to KTM producing some fine mopeds. This kept the company healthy, until the slump ended towards the end of the decade, and meant that not only were they able to return to the production of pukka motor cycles but also that they were in a strong enough financial position to start thinking about the entry of works bikes into international motocross events, a move that was to take KTM into the greatest phase of their history.

The new mopeds to come out of Mattighofen in the 1960s fell into two categories. The first of these, the Comet range, was released in 1964 and consisted of mopeds with the styling of lightweight motor cycles, powered by Sachs two-stroke 50cc engines. The other was the Hobby range and these were more in the style of conventional mopeds with step through frames and 50cc Puch power units. The latter of these two model ranges was introduced in 1967, a year which is also famous at KTM as the year when development of the motocross machines began.

Rome was not built in a day, so the old saying goes, but the story of KTM's motocross machines is one of two strikingly different halves. The development of the frame and the balance of the machine took five years to reach a truly successful formula, while the engine took only two years before it was there at the forefront of motocross competition powering KTM to their first world championship. Beginner's luck is something that we all hope for but when in 1972 KTM produced the first of their home-made engines, a 175cc, single-cylinder two-stroke unit, even they could not have prophesied that in such a short time a derivative of this design would be taking that canny Russian Gennady Moisseev to the 250cc world title.

Since this initial victory KTM has enjoyed enormous success and although they surrendered the world title, to fellow Austrians Puch in 1975, the factory managed to collect the World 250cc Manufacturers' Championship in 1976, when only brilliant riding by Finland's Heikki Mikkola, on a Husqvarna, prevented Moisseev from regaining his crown. In addition KTM riders took overall victory in the 1976 International Six-Day Trial, winning three classes outright and collecting fifty-one gold medals, thirty-four silver and five bronze. The year 1976 also brought twenty National titles the way of KTM mounted riders; these included those of the USA and Russia.

KTM was by 1976 one of the world's most forward looking motor cycle concerns with 60 per cent of all production going for export – mainly to West Germany, Italy, Switzerland, France and the USA. Sales had reached record levels and 310 motor cycles and 100 bicycles were leaving the factory daily. By mid 1977 Gennady Moisseev was well on his way to a second World Motocross title and the opportunity for further expansion at the Mattighofen works seemed to be boundless. A plan for the steady broadening of production capacity was well under way and with thirty highly skilled technicians working on research and development – such as water cooling for mopeds – the future of this successful Austrian concern was by now well assured.

One only has to look at the KTM range at the start of 1977 to find ample evidence of the company's determination to keep pace with motor cycle development. The most striking epitomisation of KTM's forward thinking was the 50cc Comet RSL. This Sachs engined machine came equipped with features hitherto reserved for the superbike rider and standard fittings included disc brakes (front and rear), tachometer, fully enclosed chain, fly screen and five spoke alloy wheels – an innovation very popular at KTM and one which is even to be found on the lowly Hobby Automatic moped.

For the 1977 World Motocross Championship the colour of the works KTMs was changed from white to red, a colour which experiment had proved was the least likely to show mud and therefore the most likely to show the factory bikes at their best as they raced to victory in motocross events around the world. An insignificant point perhaps but it is this kind of attention to detail which has led to **KTM** fulfilling the promise that was shown when Herr Kronreif and Herr Trunkenpolz joined forces in Mattighofen in 1954.   AW

Above: perhaps the best known of all KTM products are their motocross machines, the 250 and 400 models

Below: the 1971 KTM Automatic was a step-through 50cc moped with a two-stroke engine and automatic gearbox

KTM 250

Never in the history of motocross has the choice of machines been so comprehensive, nor the machines so competitive. This is particularly true of the 250cc class where any one of half-a-dozen makes, in the right hands, is a potential winner.

For any serious motocrosser contemplating the purchase of a new bike, the KTM 250 must be worthy of consideration.

The KTM 250 has been a consistent winner in motocross races around the world; indeed, Russian Gennady Moisseev won the 1974 world title on a KTM and, by mid 1977, had managed to do it again.

Moisseev, in fact, has been responsible for much of the development that has gone into the new 250, and its Grand Prix heritage is immediately apparent once the rider climbs aboard.

The KTM is powered by a single-cylinder, two-stroke, 245cc engine which develops a healthy 32bhp at 8000rpm. Ignition is by means of a Motoplat CDI unit while a 36mm Bing carburettor is fitted.

One of the KTM's strongest features is its handling. Marzocchi front forks, rated by many riders as the best currently available, have been utilised and, with no less than 8½ inches of travel, can hardly be faulted. The rear suspension is not quite so faultless but, even so, only the very fastest of riders will find it inadequate.

One of the KTM's finest points, however, is the quality of production. The Austrian company has spent a lot of time developing the 250 into a tough and reliable, yet light, machine.

Another notable KTM feature is the six-speed gearbox and the ease and precision with which it can be operated. The crisp gear change must be worth seconds to any hard-charging rider.

In all, the KTM is a serious machine for serious riders. Novices need not apply.

Engine
Air-cooled, piston port, two-stroke. 71mm (2.79in) bore × 62mm (2.44in) stroke = 245.5cc (14.97cu in). Maximum power 32bhp at 8000rpm. Compression ratio 14.1:1. One 36mm Bing carburettor. Kickstart on left-hand side.

Transmission
Multiplate clutch. Six-speed gearbox with left-hand gear change. Ratios 1st 2.57, 2nd 1.78, 3rd 1.33, 4th 1.04, 5th 0.885, 6th 0.750. Chain drive to rear wheel.

Suspension
Front – Marzocchi telescopic forks, rear – damped swinging arm.

Brakes
Drums front and rear.

Wheels and Tyres
3.00 × 21in front, 4.00 × 18in rear.

Weight
235lb (106.7kg).

Tank capacity
2.5 gals.

Seating
Single seater for race use.

Performance
Top speed around 85mph, 0–60mph in 16 secs.

THE ALTERNATIVE SOCIETY

The name Lambretta is virtually synonymous with the word 'scooter', and this sums up perfectly the position that factory has earned for itself in the 'scooter world'. Introduced and built, initially, by the giant Italian company of Innocenti SpA, at Milano-Lambrate in Northern Italy, the machines have found their way to almost every country, and built a good and strong reputation in them all.

While Europe set about rebuilding itself after World War II, the demand for economic transport became very apparent, especially to the Italians and their neighbours, and lightweight motor cycles started to appear from seemingly every little engineering works. Innocenti, however, had other ideas, to build scooters, something that would appeal to a wider circle of potential buyers. They would be cleaner to ride, allowing their riders to use them for their social trips without troubling to wear special clothing as on a motor cycle proper.

True, motor scooters had been made before, but not in the volume that the Innocenti people envisaged, and with the attendant publicity they planned. So, in 1946 the first scooters came out of the factory, they proved popular, the factory expanded, and in time built up a highly efficient mass production assembly line. Even though the scooters were well received the factory did explore the lightweight motor cycle field, and even made a prototype, vee-twin, dohc racer, but decided to revert to scooters, their really successful and specialised product. This was in the 1950 era.

By 1954, the Innocenti organisation was split into three main divisions, one making specialised machines, presses, milling machines and so on, another for the production of steel, seamless tubes etc, while the third was devoted to motor scooters and the three wheeled trucks derived from the former and used so extensively all over Italy. The way in which the Lambretta scooters developed and multiplied was helped considerably by the other divisions, which were so well attuned to the Lambretta expansion programme. Just three models of scooter were offered in 1954, all were 125ccs, and the most powerful boasted just 5bhp, but gave a fuel consumption of 140mpg (the 4bhp model was claimed to manage 193mpg!) and a top speed of 45 to 50mph. Add to this the general cleanliness, and 'acceptability' to the general public, and it was not difficult to understand why sales climbed higher ever higher. The little three-wheelers with the front of the scooter and a rear replaced by a two-wheeled load bed, found favour with everyone in business, from the baker to the local highway department, and expansion continued.

Below: a 125cc single-cylinder Lambretta model B of 1948

The production of motor scooters, three-wheelers and motor cycles in Italy had grown to more than 600,000 per year by 1956, and Lambretta were taking a healthy share of it. In fact, by 1957 the range had been extended to include the famous TV-175 scooter, and even a new 50cc Lambretta moped. The TV-175 was in line with the basic Lambretta design, with the motor forward of the rear wheel driving the rear wheel on the off-side by enclosed chain. There was a dual seat (the 150LD had separate seats, the pillion of 'swing' type) and the output was boosted to 8.6bhp. Four gears were installed, and the new model was quite a lively performer, and popular with the youngsters. Top speed was 65mph, which at the time was quite swift for a scooter of any size. The moped was, on the other hand, not a quick device, and with just 1.7bhp on tap, the top speed, through the two-speed gearbox, was only just over thirty miles per hour. There were however, trailing link forks and swinging arm rear suspension. The three-wheeler had by this time grown up from 125 to 150cc, and in addition to the three forward gears, a reverse was fitted. The rider had a cab, and even an opening roof was standard equipment. The 125cc model continued, as it had proven popular over the past years, but the 150cc motor was now the primary one in the line.

Innocenti continued to grow, and the British Austin and Morris cars started to be manufactured under licence. Massive, highly-efficient production lines were set up, and the company produced the cars and scooters in the Motor Division, while the other products continued in the other Mechanical Division, the machine tools and steel products now being merged. By the middle 'sixties, the workforce was around the 7000 mark, and on face value the future just had to be good, for Lambretta seemed to be a name that would be secure forever. However it was not to be, at least for the giant Italian producer. By 1966 the range had been extended in an effort to cater for an even greater public, the models starting at 50ccs, and going up through 98, 125, 150, 175 and 198ccs. On the scene came the LI Special models too, in both 125 and 150cc capacities, and there was also the Special X200 flagship of the scooter line. Output of that was no less than 11bhp at 5500rpm!

Top left: this competition 125cc Lambretta competed in the 1951 International Six-Days Trial event

Above left: a 150cc Lambretta model LD of 1954

Bottom left: the clean lines of Lambretta's 100cc Cento model of 1965

The general slump in two wheeler sales was already affecting many countries, but Innocenti, with the increasing range of Lambrettas now in production, seemed to be weathering the storm. In 1968, a little 39cc motorcycle came out, and in 1970 the range was even wider and more sophisticated as the market demanded. There were, for instance, the new Lui 75S and 75SL Lubematic models, with independent oiling systems, a new moped, the 48SX, but all this, sadly, was not enough; by 1972, Lambretta scooters and mopeds had ceased to roll off the Innocenti lines. Instead the company concentrated on her many other interests.

On face value, it could have been thought that this was the end of the great Lambretta, but this was certainly not the case. Such had been the demand for Lambrettas in the 'good years', that new plants to build them in other countries had been set up. One such plant of special note was called Lambretta Locomociones SA. The company, formed way back in 1952 had, by 1954, started production in a brand new factory in Eibar. Like the Italian inventors, the Spanish company concentrated on the 125cc scooters, and offered both enclosed and naked models. Sales quickly built up, and in 1959 the three-wheeler Lambrettas also came on to the scene. Just as in Italy, there were problems with the slump in sales of the 'sixties, but the scooters did stay in production, and were still being made in 1977, as the Special 150 and Jet 200.

However, the company, its name changed to Messrs Serveta Industrial SA, found it necessary to supplement the scooter production with other products, this ironically, occurring as Innocenti withdrew from scooter production. As already mentioned, Innocenti had many products to concentrate on, but the Spanish company was not so diversified. The natural progression was into the moped market, and in 1972 the Spanish offshoot announced its new range. A small one initially, it included both utility and sports type models, and was received by the Spanish public quite well. Lambretta had a good name after all, so there was no reason why its mopeds should not be every bit as good and reliable as its scooters.

Spain being very much a motor cycle minded country, there was a great potential in the younger sector of the buying populace, so in 1973 a larger and more sportingly flavoured range was offered. Mopeds for use on and off the road formed the backbone of the new Lambretta offerings, most notable being the Trepador (meaning Climber) and the Ranger.

Came 1975 and there were seven 50cc models in production, as well as the scooters. The engines, made by Serveta Industrial, were novel in that the gearboxes could be worked on easily, without the engines having to be removed from

Below: cutaway of the suspension and engine of the 75cc Lui model, with independent oiling for the engine

Bottom left: close up of the 1969 Lambretta Cometa engine

Bottom right: the 50cc Luna of 1969 was styled by Bertone of Turin

the frames. The eight disc clutches ran in oil, and gearboxes ranged from three to five speeds. Several pure roadsters were now in the line, so that the wishes of every young rider were catered for.

Late in 1975, the new 50cc Puma came on to the market; a roadster, it had a new motor which boasted a five speed gearbox, 10 to 1 compression, and a sunburst head. It was a very smart machine complete with matched speedo and revcounter. In 1977 a 'Cross' version was offered, the Puma 5V Cross, and that was an even prettier looking model. So successful is Lambretta now in the 50cc class, that there are thoughts of turning to racing. The Italian factory, it will be recalled made a prototype 250cc racer, but it was never a serious participant on the GP circuits. However, it seems likely that the Spanish factory may achieve success. Early in 1977 a new racer was unveiled, a 50cc water-cooled two-stroke with 14 to 1 compression, and a very respectable 15bhp at 15,000rpm. Fitted with alloy wheels and streamlined in the best 50cc tradition, it certainly seems to have great potential. No decision on an entry into world Championship GP racing had been made at the time of writing, but if a positive one were made, a new chapter would be written into the great name 'Lambretta'.

The scooter, being a more 'fashion conscious' vehicle than a motor cycle, must inevitably suffer more from the 'fads' prevailing from year to year, and sales graphs rise and fall, sometimes quite alarmingly, prompted by fashion's whim. However, Lambretta has succeeded in overcoming the troubles of the last few years, and looks set to remain as a name not to be overlooked in scootering, in every part of the world and for some time to come.   DJ

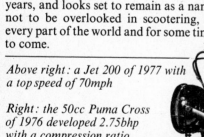

Above right: a Jet 200 of 1977 with a top speed of 70mph

Right: the 50cc Puma Cross of 1976 developed 2.75bhp with a compression ratio of 10:1

Top: a Lambretta GP200 model of late 1972. A 150cc version of the GP model was also available

Lambretta GP150

The 'modern' scooter was first conceived in 1946 and was intended as a cheap and economical form of alternative transport. During the mid 1960s they became very popular, particularly in Britain – they were a fundamental part of the 'Mods and Rockers' era – but by 1977 had lost a lot of their appeal. This was mainly due to the advent of the moped and the mass-produced lightweight motor cycle, both of which were perhaps more economical and safer to ride.

Still popular with scooter enthusiasts, however, is the Lambretta GP150. Lambretta is now part of an ever expanding and complicated empire and some Lambretta models are even built, believe it or not, in the Lucknow area of northern India.

The GP150 is one of only two Lambretta models now available in Britain and is powered by a piston port two-stroke single-cylinder engine of 148cc. Power output is a meagre 9.3bhp at 6300rpm. Fuel feed is by means of a 22mm Dell'Orto carburettor, ignition is by means of flywheel magneto and the engine's compression ratio is rated at 8.25 to one.

The engine, together with the bodywork panels and the suspension system is bolted to the GP150's underfloor spine frame. This gives it a lot of strength but also makes for extra weight and bulk which effect ultimate performance.

Performance, apart from fuel consumption, is not the GP150's strong suit. Top speed is about 60mph but acceleration is hardly earth shattering. But that really is beside the point, because scooters are intended as cheap commuter transport. In this respect the GP150 is first class, returning a fuel consumption of around 90 miles to the gallon.

Instrumentation on the GP150 is sparce. There are no indicators, nor is there a tachometer or trip mileage recorder.

The brakes fitted to the GP150 are drums front and rear and braking from 50mph to standstill takes close on 100 feet in the dry.

Although, as mentioned earlier, scooters are losing popularity, there is still a market for a machine which is easy to run, easy to keep clean and cheap on the pocket. So it is not surprising to see scooters still being manufactured. Indeed, many of the motor cyclists of tomorrow will probably owe

their initial training to the ubiquitous but often overlooked scooter.

Engine
Air-cooled, piston port two-stroke single-cylinder. 57mm bore × 58mm stroke = 148cc. Maximum power 9.3bhp at 6300rpm. Compression ratio 78.25:1. One 22mm Dell'Orto carburettor. Kickstart.

Transmission
Multiplate clutch in oil bath. Four-speed gearbox with hand clutch change. Ratios, 1st 15.4, 2nd 10.7, 3rd 7.97, 4th 5.7. Chain final drive.

Suspension
Front – trailing link, coil springs – rear, swinging crankcase and damper.

Brakes
Drums front and rear

Wheels and Tyres
3.50in × 10in front and rear

Weight
264lb (kerb)

Tank capacity
1.8 gallons

Seating
Dual saddle

Performance
Maximum speed around 60mph. Fuel consumption on average 90mpg

A Family Affair

The Lampkin brothers have been part of the trials scene for so long that it is difficult to remember the time when the sport got along without them. Arthur Lampkin, the original Mr Television of winter scrambles on the screen, is still a successful trials sidecar driver after a distinguished competition career spanning more than 20 years.

Alan Lampkin, five years younger, courageously tackled the difficult task of living up to his big brother's reputation and became one of the most stylish performers in the feet-up game.

Martin Lampkin, youngest and tallest of the Yorkshire trio, completed the family legend. British and European trials champion in 1973, and Britain's only individual world champion in motor cycling in 1975, he became the third Lampkin to win the prestigious Scottish Six Days Trial and rubbed home his superiority by doing it twice!

Never before have three brothers made such an extraordinary impact on cross-country motor cycling. For although they now specialise in trials, all the Lampkins have been motocross winners in their time.

A former 500cc motocross grand prix winner, gold medallist in the International Six Days Trial, no mean grass track racer, and a brilliant trials rider, Arthur rode into history when he won the 1963 Scottish Six Days. His speed over the boulders of Laggan Locks during his victorious ride on a 250 BSA remains one of the most unforgettable moments in the story of the Highland classic.

It was once said that Arthur John Lampkin (date of birth: 30 May 1938) was 'born on wheels'. At least that was his father's explanation when his bike-mad youngster was hauled before a magistrates' court at Skipton for riding on the road before he was old enough to have a licence.

Strangely enough, the lad who started the Lampkin legend was not born in Yorkshire. He came into the world at Shooters Hill, near Woolwich Arsenal, London, where his father, Arthur Alan Lampkin, was a foreman machine turner at the outbreak of World War II.

The family moved north in 1940, to get away from the London blitz, and settled at Silsden, near Ilkley, Yorkshire, where Arthur and Alan now run the precision engineering business their father founded. When Mr Lampkin senior first came to Yorkshire, he rode to work on an old side-valve BSA, and it was on this bike that young Arthur fell foul of the law for riding on

Right: Arthur Lampkin leaps his 500 BSA at Hawkstone Park during the 1965 British GP

the road at 15.

Arthur made his competition debut with L plates on a 197cc James. He was still a learner when he rode in the Scott for the first time, a time and observation classic he was destined to win three times. Still a regular competitor in the crazy gallop Yorkshiremen regard as 'the greatest of all trials', Arthur won in 1960 and 1961, when he achieved the ultimate of being fastest on time and best on observation. He won again in 1965.

Trials rider at 16, Arthur became the youngest-ever member of the BSA team at 17, being entrusted with a new 350 works bike for his first scramble as a reward for an excellent debut in the Scottish Six Days. His scrambles baptism was crowned by an embarrassing moment as he landed in a holly bush at the foot of Post Hill, near Leeds. His progress was so rapid, however, that, at 18, Arthur won the coveted Pinhard Prize for the year's best effort by an ACU clubman under 21.

Winner of the 250cc British moto cross championship in 1961, when he was also second in the European championship (before the series was given world status), Arthur spent many years playing second fiddle to Jeff Smith, the last Briton to win a world motocross championship. Arthur's switch to sidecar trials, with accountant Colin Pinder as passenger, was as spectacular as his hey-days as a television scrambles star. Quick to adapt to a modern Bultaco outfit, the partners became serious contenders for the British sidecar championship.

Noted for his bluntness, Arthur had always been critical of some of his rivals. In 1976, he forsook his twistgrip in favour of rugby, but he made a fine comeback in 1977, leading the national series despite a succession of protests and counter protests.

Married with three sons, Arthur had high hopes that another generation of Lampkins would be going strong by the time he quit the sport. His eldest son John has already had several schoolboy sport successes to his credit – on a Bultaco of course!

Winner of America's opening round of the 1974 world trials championship, Alan Raymond Charles Lampkin (born: 7 April 1944) is perhaps the most imperturbable of the family. Still a teenager when he scored his first national win, at the Travers Trophy trial, Alan rode for BSA, Cotton and Suzuki before he joined the Bultaco team in 1970. His initials 'ARC' sparked off the nickname 'Arc Lamp' but he is more often known as 'Sid', which nobody has ever been able to explain!

Below left: Arthur Lampkin (also pictured in the family workshop, right) leads Bryan Goss and Malcolm Davis on his 250cc Cotton at Cadwell in 1964

Below right: Arthur's 500 BSA in 1966

True to type, Alan gained his first taste of competition before he was officially old enough to ride a bike. In 1959, he went to watch Arthur struggling in the Ilkley Grand National. He was allowed to participate without actually competing. Alan got so carried away that officials had to chase him off the moors before darkness fell on Ilkla Moor Baht'at!

Content with a finisher's certificate from his first Scott, in 1961, Alan nevertheless blew off many of the established aces. In 1963, on a works BSA, he was clearly on the way to matching his brother's prowess. Winning the Bemrose and the Ilkley GN, and beating Jeff Smith at a television scramble, were landmarks in his career. 1966, however, was the big year.

Alan Lampkin won both the Scottish Six Days and the Scott, a feat very few riders have achieved in the same year.

After his sensational Scottish success, including a fantastic scrap with the legendary Sammy Miller from whom he regained the lead on the fifth day with a historic climb of Leitir Bo Fionn, then one of the most difficult hills in the trial, 'Sid' had truly arrived!

Winner of three gold medals in the ISDT, the last as a member of Britain's runner-up World Trophy team in the United States, in 1973, Alan played an inconspicuous but important part in the success story of the younger brother with whom he fought a dramatic battle for second spot in the British trials championship of 1972.

Harold Martin Lampkin (born 28 December 1950) claims his most embarrassing moment was dropping his brother's bike over the edge of a quarry. Once a serious contender for the Shell under-21 motocross championship, racing a Husqvarna, 'Mart' is now a full-time professional trials rider. At one time a partner in a coal business, he devotes all his energies to a sport which is becoming increasingly commercial.

Unable to get a licence before Christmas 1966, he competed in his first trial four days after his 16th birthday. The event was near Otley, in January 1967, and 'Mart' was the third best novice. His first national win came two years later when he won the Welsh Trophy trial on a 125cc Alta Suzuki. It was his and the bike's first major success.

In 1971, Martin became the second member of the family to win the Pinhard Prize. He had competed on a variety of machines, including BSA, Greeves and Suzuki, before he landed a Bultaco contract for 1972. His ambition was always to eclipse the

Left: Alan Lampkin in action during the 1977 European Trial

Below: Alan urges his 325cc Bultaco over the Ben Nevis section during the 1974 Scottish Six Days Trial

achievements of his brothers and he justified the faith of the Spanish factory by finishing runner-up in both the British and European championships.

In those days Martin was humping 20 tons of coal a week, during the winter, and travelling all over Europe the rest of the year. His split second reactions when tackling difficult hazards carried him to the top of the trials ladder. At the penultimate round, in Sweden, he deprived Mick Andrews of the European championship he had held for two years. On the crest of the wave, he came home to clinch his first British title. Out of luck in the international series of 1974, when the crown went to Malcolm Rathmell, Martin hit back in 1975 when he saved the self respect of the sport in Britain – in the first year the trials title carried 'world' status. In a tense climax, Lampkin finished level with Rathmell for second place behind Andrews. The outcome of the decisive round, in Czechoslovakia, rested on a count of cleans. When the punch cards were checked, Lampkin had nine more cleans and the prestige of being the world's first trials champion was his.

After trying for ten years, Martin Lampkin finally won the Scottish Six Days in 1976. He returned to defend his crown in 1977 and completely overshadowed all his rivals. PH

Right: Martin Lampkin (348 Bultaco) at the 1977 World Trial

Below left: Martin displays his style at the 1976 Mitchell Trial

Below right: Martin on his way to a 'massacre' of all others in the 1976 Scottish Six Days Trial

In the Shadow of Saarinen

When the great Finnish rider Jarno Saarinen was killed in a tragic pile-up at Monza, Italy, in May 1973, his fellow countryman and close friend, road racer Teuvo 'Tepi' Lansivuori found himself at the crossroads.

The heart-rending question Lansivuori had to ask himself was whether he should carry on racing, defending the national honour that Jarno had left behind, or whether he should quit as a token of respect.

For Saarinen had been almost half of Tepi's life as they travelled the continental circus, riding Yamahas – using his superior grasp of the English language to help Tepi through the tangle of officialdom the sport always demanded.

After serious thought and a two-month lay-off however, the little Finn with the tongue-twisting name was finally lured back by offers of competitive machinery from the Finnish importer, Ardwison.

It was a decision he later had no cause to regret. In that same year, he finished runner-up in the 350cc World Championship behind MV's Italian superstar, Giacomo Agostini, and as an added bonus, Tepi came second in the 250cc title chase too.

Lansivuori was born on 9 December 1945 at Iisalmi, 500 kilometres north of Helsinki and close to the Arctic Circle. His interest in motor cycle sport began when he was a young lad – and he took part in his first competitive event, an ice-race, on a 175cc Husqvarna in 1963. Needless to say, he won outright!

After that he tried just about everything, including motocross and even sand racing, before deciding to concentrate on road racing. His first tarmac-burner was also a Husqvarna, but when he made his Grand Prix debut in 1968, it was on a 125cc Montesa.

His first World Championship victory came in 1971 when he was a regular competitor on a Yamaha. He won the 350cc race at the Spanish Grand Prix at the end of that year.

He campaigned his bright yellow Yamahas throughout 1972, improving as a rider all the time, but he was having problems too. The first to admit that he is the world's worst spannerman, he was having to employ a mechanic, and his bike just did not have the knife-edge superiority of pukka works-supported machines. He was, however, offered a place in the Ardwison team along with

Saarinen and Matti Salonen at the end of that year – a year in which he beat Agostini for the first time in the 350cc race at the French Grand Prix, finishing second behind Jarno.

Although 1973, the year of tragedy, was good for results, Tepi suffered a series of late-season crashes and was finally treated by a Belgian specialist. Riding a 500cc Yamaha four at Mallory Park, he fell twice, and in Spain his 350cc Yamaha seized up and cast him off. He damaged an elbow which kept him out of the sport for the rest of the year. In 1974 Tepi's rise to the top was rapid. He teamed up with his former rival Giacomo Agostini to become a fully-fledged member of Yamaha's road racing squad.

The year 1974 also gave Lansivuori – who weighs just over nine stone, and is just five feet six inches tall – his first taste of 750cc riding. He soon surprised everyone by the ease with which he could fling the big, heavy water-cooled fours around the circuits. In fact his first-ever 750cc

Below: flying Finn Tepi Lansivuori in action on his 250cc Yamaha at Spa in 1973; he went on to win this race

ride was at Daytona that year – and he finished an astonishing fifth.

He found life harder in the Grands Prix. Britain's Phil Read, riding at last his dream bike, the MV Agusta, took on the challenge of the works Yamahas and robbed them of the title they so much wanted. Lansivuori had a mixed year, sometimes finishing well up, and at others suffering all kinds of problems which led to him being dubbed road racing's 'hard luck man' by the popular two-wheel press. Still, he managed to finish third in the World Championship.

The following year, he switched to the ultra-rapid Suzuki fours, and played an important part in the development of the machines which by 1977 had given Barry Sheene two world titles. On the unfamiliar Suzukis, Tepi quickly settled down, his performances sometimes overshadowed by Sheene, Read and Agostini, but at the end of the day he was always among the best, and finished third in the championship again in 1975.

He did better still in 1976 – finishing second behind Sheene – after a really hard-fought year – but that golden dream of a world championship title still eluded him.

Quiet and shy, with a blond, droopy moustache and clean limbs, Lansivuori is everyone's picture of a typical Finn. He learned to speak English at a much later date than Saarinen, who had always acted as his spokesman, and he always found it difficult to speak to journalists and organisers.

Usually accompanied by his beautiful blonde wife Helena, he can have his fellow-competitors in fits of laughter with his dry, almost deadpan sense of humour. His face gives little away by means of expression – in fact it is difficult usually to tell whether he is in a good mood or a bad one.

Before he became really embroiled in the fast-moving world of big-time motor cycle racing, Tepi's profession was, of all things, an undertaker. His father owns a coffin factory and Tepi's special responsibility was making decorations for the coffins.

He likes to spend the winter at home in Finland, and takes part in long-distance trials to keep fit. He also travels around by Snowmobile when the snow gets too deep for other modes of transport.

He began the 1977 road racing season with two machines – a 750cc Yamaha of the Life racing team, and a 500cc Suzuki, but it was not a good year. Until the

British Grand Prix in August at Silverstone, at which he finished third in the 500cc race, his best performance had been fourth in the Belgian Grand Prix.

Good times or bad, the little Finn – one of the smallest top-flight riders contesting the big classes – always manages to steal the heart of the crowds, and at his best, there are still few riders in the world who can beat him. PK

Above: the spectacular Lansivuori at Imola 1973. The machine is a TZ350 water-cooled Yamaha

Below: Lansivuori on the works 750cc Suzuki at Daytona in 1975

THE REALISTIC ROMANTICS

As a name becomes something more than a mere identity tag, it begins to mean different things to different people. Any ordinary visitor to the Turin Motor Show might suppose that Laverda were merely makers of trailer caravans, were it not for the decorative presence on the dais of a brightly-hued motorcycle, worn like a favour in the stand's buttonhole.

Some Italian farmer, seeking a new car in those elegant Nervi pavilions, might find either of these vehicle types a surprise: he would associate the Laverda name with combine harvesters. The dedicated motor cyclist could not fail to be familiar with the formidable twins and triples that compose the current range of Laverda two-wheelers; but would he know that the firm's motor cycling reputation was built on tiny commuter-bikes and strengthened with scooters?

This change in style and emphasis might be attributable to the descent of a generation, to the youthful assertiveness of brothers Massimo and Piero Laverda as they gradually took over the direction of the motor cycle factory from overall boss of the Laverda group of companies, father Francisco.

Yet it does not take a Mendeleev to see that people tend to be very much the same from generation to generation – especially Italians with motor cycling in their blood. The metamorphosis of the Laverda motor cycle was not really the play of ages, so much as a measure of the times. Doubtless today's 750 twins and 1000 triples are right for the 1970s; beyond doubt the 75 single was just right for 1949.

That was when the first production motor cycle emerged from the Laverda workshop. It was a time when romanticism had to be tempered by realism. After the war that had left Italy in chaos, it was hard enough for any kind of firm, engineering or otherwise, to struggle to its feet and maintain any kind of balance.

If the firm was venturing into vehicle manufacture, then (regardless of any previous history and irrespective of any ambitions) what it chose to offer was determined by moral obligations, albeit backed by commercial wisdom; the most dull and utilitarian transport was in a way exciting enough then, when transport was so scarce. Basic the early post-war motor cycles might be, but basic transport was all that customers could hope for, and certainly all that they could afford.

A few makers of proprietary engines catered for most of the multitude of bike-assemblers in slowly emergent post-war Italy. Laverda acquired an immediate distinction by making its own engine for the first machine. The company earned further distinction by making it well.

The 1949 *Motoleggera* (lightweight motor cycle) and its immediate successors grew to be loved as much for durability and reliability as for any dynamic virtues. There are plenty still to be seen in daily use even today, perhaps not loved so much as simply taken for granted. It may all have started off as a romance, or perhaps as a mere flirtation, with ideas in pressed steel that were engendered in America and nurtured in Europe, ideas about engines and controls that were pure-bred Italian.

The engine was a 45 × 46mm four-stroke, its stoutly-finned cylindrical barrel snugging a steel liner while all that was visible was aluminium. At 5200rpm, its specific output was 40bhp per litre, which was not bad for something tuned to run on the noisome petrol then available. It meant that the little 74cc motor could propel a rider at a steady 43mph, and that was then enough.

Laverda never stinted. There was never less than enough – in any bike they built, except the two speed scooter, to which we shall come later – and so the '75' had proper lighting, unlike so many rival runabouts. The pillion foot rests were detachable, not because they might be more than enough, but because they could be used as tyre levers. The pressed steel spine frame had a dip just under the saddle nose, the depth of the arch beneath was still enough for stiffness and stress-distribution, while the clearance above it was also enough for a skirted lady to swing a decorous leg across. The Laverda was not then a motor cycle for enthusiasts; it was a motor cycle for people.

Italian people tend to be enthusiastic, however, so it was inevitable that some *Motileggere* should be modified for competition. Laverda could see the value of racing as a publicity medium, so in 1951 the factory climbed onto the bandwagon. Mechanically the new model was no different from the old; the difference was that it looked like a motor cycle. And since Laverda never stinted, and what was enough for the *Motoleggera* might not be enough for its sporting offshoot, a pair of adjustable friction dampers were scissored onto the rear suspension.

That rear suspension might attract the attention of publicists today, if it did not then. It was what our current journalists tend to call cantilever, its basis was a trailing fork, from the pivot end of which a lever projected up to engage a laminated leaf spring concealed beneath the saddle. The dampers were not meant to stiffen the ride in the rigorous fashion then deemed appropriate to track racing; they were to quell the pitching induced by the rough roads of Italy where the great races were then run.

Right: this is the 75cc single-cylinder prototype of 1949

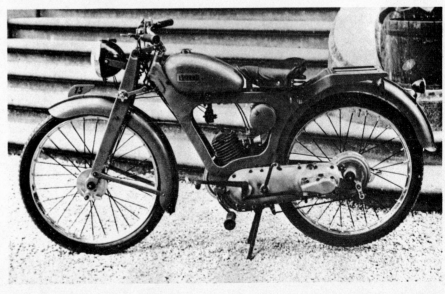

They were races over enormous distances, on public roads closed (more or less) for the event.

The *Giro d'Italia* was what it said, a tour of Italy, 1250 miles of rough tracks and back roads spread over half a dozen daily stages. The Milan–Taranto race was more straightforward, a paralysing blind down the length of Italy. Even to finish one of these events was an honour, both for rider and machine; to win was to conquer both nature and statistics, a triumph of ability and probability.

In 1951 four Laverdas started in the Milan–Taranto event, and all four finished. In 1952 a Laverda won its class, and again all Laverda starters finished. It was the beginning of a tradition in which roadworthiness counted for as much as sheer (or mere) speed – and if that was a tradition to which certain other Italian manufacturers might also be heirs, Laverda could add the blazons of quality-controlled durability to its achievement.

These heraldic fancies might have seemed a little far-fetched in distant 1952, but the facts behind them influenced the machines that came out in the following year. It was in 1953 that tubular frames took the place of pressed steel, telescopic forks the place of Webb girders, a four-speed gearbox the place of a three-speeder (still with the typically Italian and sensible rocking pedal), and a McCandless-type of rear suspension (in the image of the Manx Norton) in place of the cantilevered leaf spring which had been previously used.

It was then that Laverda started another tradition that was to reach fruitition later in the 750 SFC. They offered a sports model fully prepared for long-distance road racing. All the tricks of the tuner's trade could be played on the little 74cc engine, to such good purpose that the factory team's exemplars were said to work up to 10bhp at 13,000rpm – equivalent to 135bhp per litre, which sounds extravagant, but also equivalent to a brake mean effective pressure of 135lb sq in, which is not exceptional or unreasonable. At any rate, it was enough to sustain the little buzz-bomb in the maintenance of a 56mph average speed over 700 battered Appenine miles in the 1953 Milan–Taranto race. Once again, the winner of the appropriate class was a Laverda. So were the next

Top right: by 1951, the 75cc prototype had been developed to look like this

Above right: Laverda's 100cc single-cylinder racer of 1954

Right: the 49cc Laverdino Turismo moped model was built between 1959 and 1961; most of the early Laverdas were small lightweights

thirteen finishers. So was the class winner in the *Giro d'Italia*.

In effect, 1953 was the end of the beginning. In the years that followed, designer Luciano Zen engineered a succession of derivatives of the original Laverda lightweight, beginning with a bored and stroked version that mustered 100cc and was marketed in utility, touring and sporting versions until 1960. There were some discursions from 1958 when a two-stroke moped, curiously disc-braked, appeared in the catalogue, to be followed in 1961 by a scooter using the four-stroke engine that had been developed for an alternative moped. That scooter was by all accounts a little charmer in all respects bar one: it had a two-speed transmission, and that was at least a speed too few. The omission was rectified in 1962, and the pretty little 60cc scooter (soon to grow to 66cc) won devotees all over Europe, and even a few in Britain.

However, 1962 saw the birth of a new motor cycle, a 200cc twin incorporating much of the machinery of the old single, in a new composite chassis that was conventionally tubular and telescopic at the front, but with pressed steel backbone and hips.

Mainstay of Laverda's motor cycle business for the best part of a decade was the 200. Gradually changing the image of the company, however, came the 125 single of 1966: this was a completely new ohv engine, its cylinder horizontal beneath a multi-tubular spine flame, the whole thing being dressed as a definitely sporting job of relatively high performance, uncompromised by the grosser habits of the utility market. The quest for the best in quality led Laverda to Bosch for some electrics, to Ceriani for front forks; but already the quest for customers had led Laverda to America, where marketing convenience tempted them into the most gross of all compromises.

In America, in one shame-ridden sentence, Laverdas were sold as Garellis;

Above: Laverda's prototype 50cc moped model of 1964

Below: Pete Gibson hurls his Laverda Jota round Silverstone in 1976

if there was no kickstarter pedal, it was because Laverda fitted a one-horsepower starter motor and a 24Ah battery. The two-throw crankshaft ran in a total of five roller bearings, the overhead camshaft in four, and the five-speed gearbox was unbelievably robust, albeit given to finding false neutrals when changing down quickly.

As for the cycle parts, they began with top-grade Ceriani forks, continued with

and when that was no longer adequate, they masqueraded as American Eagle. Doubtless there is something shameful in every manufacturer's history; at least Laverda never made anything like a bad motor cycle.

Some critics might have wondered about that when the first of the big Laverdas made its rather tentative debut in 1968. It was a bad time for motor cycles, the entire European industry being then either despondent or irresponsibly complacent. Yet here was Laverda, after twenty years of tiddlers, venturing into the heroic class with something that breathed high quality, high performance, indeed high passion. The only trouble with the original 650 twin of 1968 was that it also suggested some new height in plagiarism: the public's first reaction was to deride it as a gross parody of the Honda CB77. The engine looked disgracefully (if sensibly) similar, though its engine capacity was twice as big.

Then, when the critics looked more closely, they noticed that the castings really were beautiful, that the finish of everything was superb, that the details were conceived with care and executed with love. Then, before a hundred 650s had been built, the decision was taken to bore the engine out to 750cc, and all accusations of conceptual larceny were forgotten as a team of 650 and 750 Laverda twins cleaned up the top class of the 1968 *Giro d'Italia* as convincingly as the flyweights had once dominated the bottom class.

Thus impetuously and unquestionably, the 750 Laverda took its rightful place among the élite of the world's motor cycles. Designed as a highway express, and proven in the most punishing of long-distance races, it was fast, tireless and very well behaved, a machine of connoisseur quality. The provisions of its specification were as generous as ever:

Above: Laverda's 750GT model of 1968; the engine of the 750 model started life as a 650 unit, which was then enlarged to give more power

a massive taper-roller steering head, and developed into a convergent-divergent quadrilateral of tubes that composed a spinal frame linking the steering head and the rear fork pivot. It was an arrangement unlikely to be upset by all the urge of that torque-rich engine, or even the pull of the three big Grimeca drum brakes – though those drums were not the best, and it was possible for a hard-trying rider to induce fade. Laverda

later substituted their own drums, which were about as good as drums could be, and from their slogan for super brakes (*Syper Freni*) came the now famous SF code for the 1971 sports model.

Before that there had been the GT model, clearly a tourer, and the S which

Above: a Laverda 3C of 1975; it was powered by a 1000cc double overhead camshaft, three-cylinder motor

Below: Jeff Wade in action during the Formula 750 TT event of 1972 on his twin-cylinder Laverda 750

was set up for fast roadwork and racing. The GT was to remain on the stocks with few changes over the years, turning up now and then as a police bike; but the S underwent changes galore. This was not so much because of any weaknesses in its specification, but because its strengths were such that the temptation grew each year for owners to enter ever more strenuous competitions. The endurance races were getting much tougher and the competition more forbidding: the Japanese giants were spending lavishly, the European specialists were playing every trick in the book, and everybody who could build a big banger was flinging it into contention over durations that could range from 500km to 24 hours.

Below left: the two-stroke 2TR off-road model of 1977

Below: Laverda's three-cylinder 1000cc dohc engine is a masterpiece of engineering, producing 80bhp

Bottom: the mighty and magnificent Laverda 3CL 1000 model of 1977

A well-prepared street machine was no longer enough, Laverda had to emulate the others, with proper special-purpose machinery. They had done it before, with the 74cc sports model; in 1971 they did it again with the 750 SFC, and wiped the floor with the opposition in the endurance races of that year.

The SFC was really a bit too rorty and naughty for the road. The SF was gradually improved to match it in all but sheer speed while remaining perfectly practical for the public highway. While growing more powerful (it went up steadily from 60 to 65bhp) it also grew quieter, and alas a little heavier – not that a machine so generously endowed with strength and stiffness could ever be really light.

At best the sporting 750 scaled 480lb; at worst (or at length, however you like to look at it) it could weigh 520. Its speed was not suffered to diminish: any good S or SF could do at least 115mph when properly run in, and 118 was often nearer the mark. As for stopping the greater weight, the problem disappeared when the SF2 came on the scene with the option of two – instead of one, which was inadequate – front discs by Brembo. Two years later, in 1976, the SF3 came along with three disc brakes.

In the first half of the 1970s, Laverda were developing something that was to be a goer and a half. The same arithmetic applied, the new bike had three cylinders. Between them they encompassed a displacement of a whole litre, and the writers who tripped out to the factory at Breganze, near Venice, expressed all the wide-eyed amazement that could be provoked by an even bigger banger housed in a bicycle actually lighter than the 750. Their reports glowed as they related the prodigious power of the thousand three; somehow they never made enough of the fact that when they went out on their rhapsodic neck-wringing sessions on the 3C, they were invariably kept close company by a factory rider on a 750. . . .

In fact the three-cylinder machine turned out to need a lot of work on it – not only on the part of the rider, his right hand perpetually busy turning the twistgrip both ways, but also by the development engineers. The conical couple developed by a crankshaft with three crankpins set 120 degrees apart, created vibration problems that the (perhaps disappointingly) conventional frame could not properly handle, so it was rebalanced with the outer pins spaced 180 degrees from the inner, establishing a firing order which looked and sounded like a four-cylinder engine with one plug shorted. As for the ignition, that was a masterpiece of modern elec-

tronic science by Bosch, and it caused inordinate trouble for a couple of years.

Gradually, however, the bugs were ironed out, though too late for some irate customers who felt that they had been used as development drivers. The 3C became a bike that could really be used, and as its evolution proceeded, its glamour became recognised. Along with its flat crank and its revised electrics, it grew the two or three discs of the later SFs, together with the cast light-alloy wheels that Laverda made themselves. They are good at that kind of detail: other manufacturers in Italy use the same Brembo calipers and discs for example, but only Laverda bothered to fix those iron annuli to light-alloy spiders so as to minimise unsprung weight. Only Laverda takes the trouble to supply universally adjustable handlebars featuring radial serrations in four places to give (with the clamps) three degrees of freedom and a virtual infinity of settings.

Laverdas used to be demonstrably superior in their handling too. The S and SF series of 750s were but the 1000 can show the cloven hoof. It has had a confused history of allergies to various tyres, and on an injudiciously chosen set it can

Below: the much modified three-cylinder Laverda 1000 of Mead/Tompkinson racing in a long distance endurance event

be figuratively (and doubtless literally) mortifying at a mere 80mph, which is absurd. On the right combination it can be taut, steady and stable even at speeds of up to 135mph.

Not every 3C is that fast. Like the 750, the 1000 has done the Darwinian thing, and has branched out into mildly specialised variants. Today's 3CL is a quiet and flexible 80bhp tourer, though in its 125mph capability and high-speed swervability it is streets away from the traditions of sit-up-and-beg rubbernecking. Streets away, again, is today's Jota, a 90bhp noisemaker that may not win all that many races but is furious enough in standard form to be probably the fastest motor cycle in full production anywhere in the world.

Beyond the Jota, if the trend it demonstrated was prolonged, might lie nothing more than the law of diminishing returns. That would not do for the Laverda organisation of today, with its new modern factory and its burgeoning orderbooks. Instead, the firm has put its faith in the lore of returning diminution: the new 500 Laverda twin, as nimble as it is handsome, promises to carry the firm's reputation to new heights, though obviously not to greater ones.   LJKS

Right: the magnificent overhead-camshaft twin-cylinder engine of Laverda's 750SF model

Below: the racy lines of a 1976 Laverda SF750 machine

500 Alpina

There is an adage in the motor cycling world that 'a good little 'un is better than a good big 'un'. The Italian industry seems to have taken that to heart of late and produced a variety of mouth watering 500s, all different in character and looks. Moto Guzzi have their shaft-drive vee-twin, Ducati their desmodromic cafe-racer-styled bike, Benelli their Honda-style four and Morini their rare and delicate longitudinal vee-twin.

To compete, Laverda, from their new factory just below the hills north of Vicenza in Northern Italy, built a parallel twin with twin overhead camshafts and four valves per cylinder.

Compared to its famed stablemates, the Laverda 500 is quite reserved in looks, its conservative appearance masking a thoroughbred motor cycle with an excellent performance.

From its 496.47cc engine there is a wealth of power, peaking at 44bhp at 10,300rpm, which gives the bike a top speed of 119mph. Acceleration from a standing start to the quarter mile post takes just 13.9secs, while fuel consumption works out at a shade under 50mpg. The bike's engine is quite smooth for a four-stroke twin and the power is always there on tap: it does not suddenly come on cam and surprise the rider as he slips back on the saddle. Strangely for such a large capacity bike, the 500 uses a six-speed gearbox, but that is

something which should bother few people, if any at all! One small point, however, is that first gear is very low and there is a long gap to second.

At 377lb dry, the Laverda is not the lightest of bikes but once on the move that is quickly forgotten and one can start enjoying a very sweet handling machine indeed. From bank to bank, the 500 responds with no hesitation and one has to lean a long way indeed before anything gets in the way of the cornering. Even though the frame is of single-loop construction, it seems remarkably rigid and well able to cope with the power.

Braking is by way of three cast-iron Brembo discs which work well in all weathers.

Pedal and lever pressure was found to be a little on the high side, however. Alloy wheels come as standard wear and are plain but pleasing to the eye.

If the thought of Italian bikes puts you off because of their unenviable reputation for finish and switchgear, the Laverda is well worth a look at. Instruments are by the Japanese Nippon-Denso company and are neat, reliable and in the right places. The standard of finish is exemplary on the bike, the welding is neat and the chrome plating good. That would come as no surprise if one were to see the clinical neatness and cleanliness of the Laverda factory at Breganze.

It is nice to ride a bike with flat bars in these days of high rise units fitted to so many

Japanese bikes, and high speed touring is very comfortable with the 500. In fact, apart from the inevitable twin-cylinder vibrations, the whole bike is comfortable and easy to live with.

The deciding factor is that, although the Laverda 500's price is comparable with those of its native competitors, that may be half as much again as rivals from the Far East, which brings us to the other saying 'You get what you pay for'.

Engine
Air-cooled twin-cylinder four-stroke. 72mm (2.83in) bore × 61mm (2.40in) = 497.46 cc (30.328cu in). Maximum power (DIN) 44bhp at 10,300 rpm; maximum torque (DIN) 33lb ft at 5200rpm. Light-alloy cylinder block and head. Compression ratio 9:1.4 valves per cylinder operated directly by twin overhead camshafts. 2 roller inner and two ball outer main bearings. 2 Dell' Orto carburettors. Electric start.

Transmission
Wet-multi-plate clutch and six-speed gearbox. Ratios 1st 16.9, 2nd 9.9, 3rd 8.6, 4th 6.9, 5th 6.5, 6th 6.1:1. Chain drive to rear wheel.

Suspension
Front – telescopic forks, rear – telescopic swinging arm.

Brakes
Twin discs front, single disc rear.

Wheels and Tyres
3.50in × 18in front, 3.50 × 18in rear.

Weight
377lb (171.5kg).

Tank capacity
3.2gals (14.5 litres).

Seating
Double saddle.

Performance
Maximum speed 119mph. Acceleration standing start quarter mile 13.9secs. Fuel consumption approximately 49mpg.

Jota

The Laverda Jota is based on the famous three-cylinder 1000cc series of machines which has, for a few years, been Italy's answer to the wave of Eastern 'superbikes'.

The specially tuned Jota is one of the quickest production motor cycles available. To add to that distinction, it is also one of the tallest and noisiest machines available.

Apprehension and perhaps even fear are feelings that enter a rider's head when the Jota is first seen waiting to be mounted and ridden. With the excellent adjustable bars at their low, almost racing, setting and the pegs high up the frame, the whole machine looks awesome. The massive engine and gearbox casing do little to make the rider feel easier. With

the bike off the centre stand (there is no side stand for the timid or weak!) and on the move, however, the whole feeling changes.

If pottering around town is your fancy, the pencil-slim machine will manoeuvre in and out of traffic with ease; when you stop, you can wait quite a few seconds before you have to lower the landing gear – or at least it seems that way as the Laverda is such a well balanced bike. Nevertheless, buy a Jota and ride in town and you are showing the world how you

waste your money.

Not even motorways are the true domain of this creature, for it longs for the country road where it can show its abilities off to the full.

The acceleration is out of this world, as one would expect with 90bhp being churned out by the odd configuration engine (the two outer cylinders are at TDC when the middle is at BDC, which means the engine misses a beat after every three firings). The Laverda Jota should, and does, cover a standing start

quarter mile in 12.1secs, tops
137mph and return 38mpg. On
the road, the performance
seems much greater than that.
Along with a deafening
crescendo of noise, the bike
thrusts forward with amazing
power and speed. Changing
from first to second is hard
(and into neutral nearly
impossible at standstill), but
thereafter changes can be
swift and precise. Here another
fault comes to light: there are
no mirrors as standard, which
is annoying at the least and
dangerous when travelling at
high speed – as you would be
now had you given the bike
full throttle when this sentence
started!

Handling on such a large
(475lb) bike is remarkable: it
banks over without hesitation
and once down, does not twitch
or move off line, bumps or no;
the TT100 Dunlop tyres have a
lot to do with this. The brakes,
three discs, are superb but they
are a bit heavy; the back brake
had some play in it but that
was probably just a fault of
our test bike.

Apart from the adjustable
(in four places) bars, the pegs,
the left-foot brake, the front
brake lever and the right-foot
gearchange can all be placed
for personal taste. If you prefer
the Japanese/American
gearchange, a conversion kit
can be supplied.

Perhaps the biggest criticism
of the bike was its touring
capabilities, for the seat was
very thin and uncomfortable;
the pillion too was perched too
high. Touring and passenger
carrying are not the forté of the
Jota, however, for it is a mean
machine which calls for an
experienced rider on his own –
not to tame it but to live with
it happily.

Engine
Air-cooled three-cylinder
four-stroke. 75mm (2.95in)
bore × 74mm (2.91in) stroke =
980cc (59.80cu in). Maximum
power (DIN) 90bhp at
7250rpm. Light-alloy cylinder
block and head. Compression
ratio 10:1. 2 valves per
cylinder operated directly by
twin overhead camshafts. 3
Dell' Orto carburettors.

Transmission
Wet-multi-plate clutch and
five-speed gearbox. Ratios 1st
1.2618, 2nd 1.1883, 3rd 1.373,
4th 1.1173, 5th 1.1:1. Chain
drive to rear wheel.

Suspension
Front – telescopic forks, rear –
telescopic swinging arm.

Brakes
Twin discs front, single disc
rear.

Wheels and Tyres
4.1in × 18in front, 4.25in × 18in
rear.

Weight
475lb (215.9kg).

Tank capacity
4.37gals (20 litres).

Seating
Double saddle.

Performance
Maximum speed 137mph.
Acceleration standing start
quarter mile 12.1secs. Fuel
consumption approximately
38mpg.

Mert the Dirt

Few racing motor cyclists can claim to have co-starred with Steve McQueen on the silver screen, but Bruce Brown's film 'On Any Sunday' showed Mert 'The Dirt' Lawwill on his 100,000 mile trek to regain the AMA Grand National Championship that he won in 1969. That was Mert's year, he finished 23 out of 25 races, scored points in 19, and won four races to take the National Championship title.

Born in San Francisco, Mert started racing in 1960 under the auspices of Dudley Perkins who was still his sponsor in 1977. After three years of competition, he qualified as an expert and made it into the top ten of the end-of-year championship ratings, a position he maintained until winning the 1969 championship. As the film showed, a string of mechanical failures ruined any chance he may have had of retaining his title in 1970. In fact victory eluded him completely until Ascot (California) in 1972.

The first opportunity that Europeans had of seeing Mert in action was not, of course, where he was most at home, on the mile and half mile ovals of American dirt track, charging his XR750 Harley-Davidson sideways through bends, slipping and sliding at over 100 miles an hour. No, they saw him at Imola for the 200 miles road race in 1973. Unfortunately, poor handling wrecked any chance Mert had to qualify. He had better luck, however, in England, during the Easter Match Races of '73 when he replaced the injured Mark Brelsford and finished eleventh highest scorer, tying with Barry Sheene on 39 points. Not bad going for a dirt track specialist who had never raced in the rain before.

Mert Lawwill best displayed his skill in the American Mile Dirt Track races which took place on the hard-packed rutted clay of the fair ground trotting tracks in America's Mid-West. Typical of these, and the best, is the San José Mile. In May 1964, Mert arrived with his Harley-Davidson XT750 after weeks of engine testing with the legendary C. R. Axtell on his dynamometer. Mert qualified fastest, a full second under the lap record. He won his heat but from pole position in the final he burnt his rear tyre and slipped, smoking, into sixth position as the tyre disintegrated and eventually broke up completely.

This typified Mert's championship attempt through 1974, a season cut short by injury. The downward slide followed him into 1975 where, at his favourite track, San José, he again won his heat but finished fourth in the final as his engine failed. 1976 was a year best forgotten as he scored only five championship points from races at Harrington (Delaware) and Colombus (Ohio).

Mert's retirement was rumoured at the end of 1976 after he had spent the year receiving treatment for an inner ear complaint which affected his balance. The rumour was unfounded, although by 1977 he tended to pick his races and spent much time tuning engines for, and coaching, his protégé Mike Kidd. Kidd finished eleventh in the 1976 AMA Camel Pro Grand National Championship. If Mert was to contest only one meeting a year, it would, of course, have to be the San José Mile.

In May 1977, he put his 17 years' experience to good effect, putting in a qualifying lap time which was under national champion Jay Springsteen's lap record of the previous spring. Mert should have won his heat and qualified easily for the final, but he failed to make the first three as his exhaust system came adrift.

By one of the quirks of American racing, the first two in a consolation race also qualify. In this race Mert's swinging arm bearings broke, dropping him out of contention. Mert did not even have the satisfaction of seeing a team victory. Mike Kid, running away with the final, suffered identical bearing failure with six laps to go. Mert, an inseparable part of America's dirt racing scene should continue to thrill crowds and pass on his experience for many seasons to come.   PC

Below: Mert Lawwill in action on his 750cc Harley-Davidson at a cold and rainy Mallory Park at Easter 1973. He was competing in the Transatlantic series, the only occasion on which Lawwill has been seen in Britain; he eventually finished in eleventh place with 39 points to his name, tying with Barry Sheene

Above: Lawwill at Brands Hatch during the Transatlantic series of 1973. Lawwill, the American national champion in 1969, proved to be a very useful road racer, although he was much better known as a dirt track rider; indeed, it was on the oval dirt circuits of America that Lawwill won his title

Whatever the reasons for buying a motor cycle or moped, the advantages are manifold. A two-wheeler provides cheap reliable transport, the chance to get out into the country where bus and train routes cannot reach, but above all, it makes the rider totally independent.

There are few 'bad' motor cycles on the roads today, but some are more suited to a specific purpose than are others. The range confronting the novice rider is bewildering, but a choice has to be made before learning can begin.

Starting with the simple moped, which can achieve sometimes staggering fuel consumption figures, the rider will have to prepare himself for a slow, but extremely cheap basic transport. He will also be the subject, because of a basic lack of speed and acceleration, of severe 'carving up' by thoughtless car drivers.

Next in the choice of machine is the sports moped, already very popular with younger riders, offering a fair turn of speed with remarkable economy. Legislation, in Britain at least, has put an end to these machines for 16-year olds, and replaced them with machines which must not exceed 30mph, making for a 'sitting duck' situation for car drivers and the like.

In some countries, mopeds can be ridden without a driving licence, regard-less of performance. Many countries, however have a standard driving test for motor cyclists, and whatever test is passed, it is wise to start on a suitable machine and not run before you can walk.

The 'Trail' bike, a pseudo scrambles machine, has caught the imagination of the two-wheeled public, and the sight of these machines, with their high, wide handlebars, large wheels with knobbly tyres, and noisy exhausts is quite common. These bikes, although offering excellent manoeuvrability, have their drawbacks. The tyres, which offer off-road grip, can become slippery in the wet due to the knobblies 'walking'. Nevertheless, these machines are good fun if you have the opportunity to take them on the rough and out of harm's way.

Perhaps the best machine to start on is a 250cc model. Although this may seem too potent for a beginner, with good training, the novice rider can enjoy himself safely. There is no doubt that without adequate training, the rider can turn his motor cycle into a lethal weapon, giving weight to the cry that 'all motor cycles are dangerous'. If a rider starts on a machine which is too small, then once he has mastered it, he is likely to get bored, and so try to ride the bike to its limit, which is asking for a great deal of trouble.

From the Beginning...

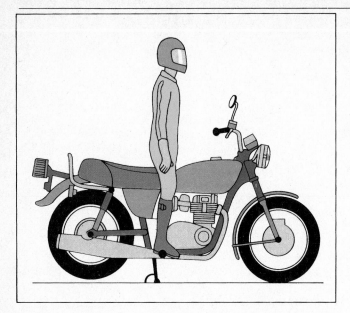

Defensive riding is probably the answer, and it is usually the best way to keep alive! Novice riders should think that all other road users are out to kill them – and at least if an accident becomes inevitable they will be prepared for it and can take evasive action.

It is essential for the rider to bear in mind that only *he* really cares for his own safety, and he is unlikely to get much help from other road users. Car drivers in particular, tend to think their paintwork is more valuable than the life of a motor cyclist. So it is a case for looking after 'number one'.

The final choice of machine should be carefully thought out, and if a decision is difficult, a compromise must be reached. A 250cc bike will have terrific acceleration and a top speed approaching 90mph. It will also be noisier, harder to ride, and cost more to run and insure than a smaller capacity machine. Equally, it can be a mistake to buy a bike that is too tame,

because with today's traffic jams, a bit of power is essential for any progress. Running costs must be borne in mind, because that flashy sports bike could present the owner with some equally flashy bills for spares and repairs. The prices and availability of spares are also factors that insurance companies bear in mind when quoting a premium for a motor cyclist.

In the smaller class of machine, the Japanese manufacturers offer a huge and comprehensive range, from sporty lightweights to practical commuting bikes. There can hardly be a country in the world today that does not import Japanese bikes, so the new and second-hand markets are well stocked.

The prospective buyer should make sure that a dealer for the make in mind is not too far away, because if anything goes wrong, there is little point in travelling too far by public transport. By finding out the prices for spares such as a

Above left: to find the ideal riding position stand upright on the pegs – with the bike on its centre stand – sit down, with back straight, and lower the arms on to the handlebars, thus leaning forward naturally and comfortably

Above right: on wet roads, extra grip can be gained by leaning inwards relative to the bike (top), while sitting upright and leaning the bike to a considerable angle can be an advantage on rough surfaces, as is ably demonstrated by the top riders on the motocross circuits of the world as well as speedway riders

clutch, a headlamp assembly, cables and a silencer, a reasonable idea of running costs can be obtained.

Whatever bike is bought, it must be safe. There is no problem with safety on a new bike, but a second-hand one should be checked. It is a good move to take along a motor cyclist friend, or better still a qualified engineer. He will be able to spot excessive wear on tyres, brakes, engine, gearbox etc.

The bike must be comfortable, because a tired rider is a dangerous one. If an uncomfortable bike is ridden for any length of time, fatigue sets in, concentration slips and bike and rider become an accident looking for somewhere to happen. The bike should have fairly straight and high handlebars, to give an upright riding position. The controls – the handlebar levers and foot pedals – should feel easy to use and naturally placed. Finally, it must be possible for the rider to put both feet on the ground.

Before setting out onto the road, it is necessary to get the right clothing and equipment. In many countries it is a legal requirement to wear a crash helmet, which must reach a certain standard of safety.

It cannot be stressed enough that a crash helmet is the only way of preventing serious head injury in the event of a crash. If a crash is too severe it may not help anyway, but thousands of riders owe their lives to crash helmets. There are many different makes of helmet on the market and, here again, it all depends on the rider's personal preference. There are two basic types, the open-face, known as jet style, and the full-face or integral helmet.

Many riders who use their machines for off-road riding, prefer the open-face style because it doesn't mist up and the range of vision is good, but of course there are drawbacks, because the face can be exposed to injury in the event of a spill. The full-face helmet is fast gaining popularity and this why such helmets can now cost much less than when the type was first introduced.

The novice rider will need some

suitable clothing and, depending on the climate in which he lives, a waterproof suit is nearly always a must. These are now very compactly made and do not need much storage space. Once again, there are advantages and disadvantages of buying one or two-piece suits. A one-piece is difficult to put on quickly and usually has fewer pockets than a two-piece, but it is often less leaky.

A two-piece suit has the advantage of being easy to put on and sometimes has more pockets, but the wind and rain can creep into it, making long journeys uncomfortable.

If an open-face helmet is purchased, then a good pair of shatterproof goggles

Top: beware of broken glass on the roads – a blow-out can be very dangerous

Left: a learner rider being taught to manoeuvre his machine through a series of tight, slow turns

techniques were different. Bikes had poor brakes and roadholding and the roads were far less crowded.

If the new rider cannot get to a training course, the following advice could help: It must be remembered that many a fool can ride a bike quickly – but it takes a good rider to ride quickly *and* safely.

Try to persuade a friend who has a full licence to take you and the bike to a plot of flat waste ground. A motor cyclist must understand road surfaces, because the average area of a motor cycle tyre that is touching the road is smaller than the size of the palm of a hand. Adhesion, therefore, is all-important.

The novice rider must be aware of sudden changes in the road surface such as white road lines, zebra or pelican crossings, pot holes, drain and manhole covers, sand, gravel, soil and mud. He should look out for patches of oil and for road flotsam – pieces of wood, metal, or tyre and nuts and bolts – because these can cause serious wobbling which can bring a bike and its rider down almost instantly.

A shower of rain can throw a completely different light on a familiar road by making it slippery. It is worth remembering that if the rain has kept off for some weeks and a sudden deluge arrives, the roads will be at their most treacherous, having built-up a layer of grease and tar, normally washed away with regular showers.

Next, the new rider should familiarise himself with his machine, and it is advisable that he reads thoroughly any handbook that the manufacturers supply. This is always supplied with a new machine, but motor cycle dealers often have handbooks of several other machines, even if the machines are out of date.

Luckily, over the years, most manufacturers have made the control layout of their machines standard, so in theory, the rider can switch from one machine to another and have an immediate understanding of the controls.

For the typical motor cycle, the controls are usually laid out as follows: front brake – lever on right-hand handlebar, rear brake – pedal operated by the right

are a must, and if the preference is for a full-face helmet, then it is a good idea to buy anti-mist cloth or liquid.

Boots are an advantage, particularly if the rider plans to travel a lot in town. The feet have constantly to be lifted up and down and the bottoms of trousers can get caught in the footrests, which is dangerous. Also, a pair of leather gloves is sensible. So, the bike is purchased, suitable clothing and equipment are worn and the new rider has to face the moment of truth – just how does he ride a motor cycle?

There is really no substitute for formal training, and many local authorities run schemes of their own or in conjunction with motoring organisations. The local branch office of one of the motoring organisations should be able to tell the novice about a suitable local motor cycle training course.

Many riders, however, live miles from any formalised training schemes, and have to rely on the help of friends, relatives or even perhaps a book.

A problem with learning from friends is that they may not take the training seriously, and although the new rider's antics may cause great hilarity, any serious tuition may take time. Another problem crops up if taking tuition from an older friend or father. It is probable that when they learnt to ride, the

Top: before attempting to ride his new machine, the learner should paddle it round for some time while he accustoms himself to the weight

Right: rehearsing arm signals in preparation for a right turn

foot; clutch – lever on the left handlebar, throttle – twist grip on the right-hand side of the handlebar.

The electrical controls are now almost completely standardised and are as follows: on the left handlebar is the horn button, light switch and indicator switch, and on the right is the starting button (if fitted) and sometimes the light on/off switch.

Even some of the smaller Japanese machines are equipped with a rev counter in addition to a speedometer. The rev counter helps prevent the rider from over-straining the engine as there is usually a red line to indicate maximum permissible revs.

On the speedometer, there are coloured lights for warning of particular functions. Usually a blue light means that the full-beam of the headlight is working, selection of neutral is indicated by a green light, whilst indicator tell-tales are usually amber.

The choke control, which is sometimes needed to start the engine, is fitted either to the handlebar, or – more likely – on or near the carburettor.

The ignition switch is usually fitted between the speedometer and the rev counter and the kick-start is usually on the right-hand side of the engine. Some European manufacturers, however, place the kick-start on the left-hand side. The gear lever is usually situated on the bottom left-hand side of the gearbox and crankcase cover.

One of the British training organisations recommends that even before the engine is started, the bike should be 'paddled' around by the new rider, to get experience of the weight of the bike. This is excellent advice, and the new rider should paddle the bike in perhaps a figure of eight. A slope should be found because that can be used to let the bike run down, and the brakes can be tried out. If a bicycle is the only other two-wheeler that has been ridden, the brakes of a motor cycle will seem tremendously powerful.

The front brake is the real stopper on a motor cycle, but it should be used in conjunction with the rear, and preferably a split second before. Once the rider is satisfied that he can handle the weight, then the next procedure is to start the engine.

Sit astride the bike, and check with the left foot that the gear lever is in neutral. This can be done without turning the ignition on, and the bike should be rocked backwards and forwards, off the stand, until the bike is in neutral.

Next, turn the petrol tap to the 'on' position, and turn on the choke if the engine is cold or has not been started for some time. Switch the ignition on, opening the throttle slightly, and if an electric starter is fitted, a quick touch of the button usually brings the engine into life instantly. If the engine does nothing, this may be caused by the 'kill' button on the handlebar being left in the 'off' position.

If you need or prefer to use the kick-start, then place the lever in the start position, put the instep of the foot over the start lever and, using a small amount of throttle, kick the lever downwards. Repeat this until the engine starts. Try not to open the throttle too much, because apart from making a lot of noise, and putting the new rider ill at ease, it doesn't do the cold engine any good. The choke, if it has been needed, will not be necessary after a few minutes running.

Above: always remember to look over your shoulder before attempting to pull off from standstill

Left: beware of raised white painted lines, such as the zig-zag ones shown here, in wet weather; they are usually slippery

Pull the clutch lever, which is used to connect and disconnect the power from the engine to the back wheel towards the handlebar. Gently press the left foot downwards (or sometimes upwards) on the gear lever, into first gear. The green neutral light will then go out.

It is possible to push the bike along even in gear so long as the clutch lever is held against the handlebar. Find out when the clutch is 'biting' by letting it out from the handlebar slowly. When this is done, the machine will begin to move off. This should only be done if the mirrors have been checked for correct positioning and the road is clear for the rider to move off.

While the clutch is being 'let out', the throttle opening should be increased, until, gradually, the machine will move off. For the absolute beginner, there is no objection to the feet sliding along the ground, because this will aid balance and confidence. The faster the machine goes, the easier it is to balance.

Once the art of moving off is mastered, braking is the next item to perfect. There will be no need to change gear at this stage, just get used to moving off and stopping correctly. To change into the next gear, the starting procedure is simply repeated, but this can be carried out a little quicker, only after the rider feels confident enough. The throttle has to be closed before the clutch is pulled in and the next gear, which is usually one notch upwards, is selected. The clutch is let out, the throttle opened again, and the machine will move away. Only plenty of practice will perfect this.

Remember, try to carry out all these exercises before venturing out onto the open road. When you have learned to change gear and brake safely, you should be ready for the open road – and try to keep to quiet side roads. You should practice moving off, and should look over your shoulder at least once – and preferably a proper look, not a brief, cursory glance.

Despite the modern machine being fitted with indicators, it is good practice to use hand signals, returning the relevant arm to the handlebars as soon as it is safe. The new rider should make every effort to keep his eyes on the road, and not look down to see how he is changing gear. Otherwise he might find himself face to face with an oncoming vehicle or parked car!

It is well to remember that the police use three basic thoughts to keep them out of harm's way: Be in the *right* position, travelling at the *right* speed, and be in the *right* gear. Bearing this in mind, the novice rider can only improve by constant practice, by undivided attention to the roads, by regular maintenance of his machine, and by using basic common sense.   GA

Below: other hazards that the learner rider needs to be wary of are drain covers, particularly when wet, and any other 'foreign' substances such as chalk

Mr Norton said No

Believe it or not, the first Levis was made in the Norton works. This strange fact was revealed by Rem Fowler, the TT ace who worked there at the time young Bob Newey – one of Norton's bright boys – first introduced his invention to the boss.

Newey approached Mr Norton after working on a small bike. Norton had just returned from one of his trips and was buttonholed by Newey, who intimated that the works had a surprise for him. To Newey's dismay Norton dismissed the small two stroke bike. 'Take it away,' said Mr J. L. Norton, 'I don't want to see it again – we only make men's bikes here'.

Newey was downhearted – he was so sure that a lot of people would have been interested in a small bike. Around the time it so happened that Bob Newey was interested in a young lady – which was a stroke of luck as she had two brothers who were later to play a part in the making of the Levis. Daisy Butterfield and brothers Arthur and Billy lived in Stechford, a suburb of Birmingham. Newey called on Miss Butterfield with his brainchild of a motor cycle.

The brothers agreed that such a grand little bike must be a commercial success, 'So why not let us start to make it?'. Mrs Butterfield, mother of the three children, arrived on the scene and was most eager to learn of the proposal. It was she who suggested the name for the bike – Levis, the Latin word for light, and no-one could deny this was a light machine. The Butterfield brothers went into business making the Levis, Bob Newey joined them and eventually Daisy Butterfield became Daisy Newey. Thus the Levis company was born.

The company hummed with ideas, using both horizontal and vertical two-stroke singles and twins. The two-stroke

Below: Arthur Butterfield's 350cc Levis being refuelled during the 1913 Junior TT held at the Isle of Man. Butterfield went on to finish thirteenth at an average speed of 36.50mph

had been invented by a Mr Day some twenty years before but, apart from Scott, no-one seemed interested in its development. Levis tried various ratios of bore and stroke until, around 1912, they evolved the classic 'Baby' Levis of 211cc with a bore and stroke of 62 × 70 mm. This little engine was a milestone in Levis history and remained in the catalogue until 1926.

Bob Newey was development engineer/ rider, competing with the Butterfield brothers in races, hill climbs and fuel consumption tests. It was Newey who discovered that two-stroke racers were faster with an expansion chamber in place of an open pipe and all Levis works racers had this then unusual fitment. Levis was of the opinion that competitions were good publicity and a team of 350cc machines were entered for the 1913 Junior TT. In 1913 there was no 250cc race, so a new engine was developed. This was a 75 × 79mm, 349cc unit fitted with twin sparking plugs.

The riders were Arthur Butterfield, Albert Milner and Bob Newey, but the venture was not a success; Newey retired with mechanical trouble on the first lap, Milner's machine caught fire and

Arthur Butterfield finished thirteenth, at 36.50mph, being the only single-speed machine to complete the course. The following year three more machines were entered, but again results were disappointing. Milner retired, Phil Pike finished thirteenth at 39.70mph and J. Veasey finished 30th at 28.3mph.

During World War I, the Butterfields continued with a small production of motor cycles – all 211cc single-geared Populars, wonderful little bikes that could be paddled off and which would run with minimum attention. When the TT races were resumed in 1920, a silver cup was offered for the best performance by a 250cc machine. Levis developed the 67 × 70mm, 247cc machine, fitted with a three speed gearbox, which must have been the best 250cc in the world. They could beat all the 350cc bikes of that period with the exception of the invincible AJS. The 250 class was Levis's domain. At half distance, R. O. Clark was in second place and may even have won the race if he hadn't crashed on the very last lap, doing great harm to himself and his machine. After a delay of ten minutes he rode in at a slow speed to finish fourth overall. The result was a triumph, with

Levises finishing first, second and third in the 250cc class.

In 1921 a Levis machine finished second in the 250cc class, the rider being G. S. Davison, the most famous Levis rider of all time. Davison rode in drill trousers, stockings and running pumps, which enabled him to run easily alongside his machine, up the hill at the Gooseneck. The other Levis riders finished fourth and eleventh. For 1922, there was a separate race for the 250cc machines and G. S. Davison romped home an easy winner on his 248cc 62 × 82.5mm Levis, thirteen minutes ahead of the second man. These were great days for the company, but fortune never smiled again on the Levis boys in the Isle of Man. The ohv engines of their competitors became more and more reliable each year and it was sixteen years before another two-stroke machine would win the Lightweight Trophy.

For 1921, the Levis production range included a 247cc model and the little 211cc 'Baby'. A two-speed gearbox was also available. In reliability trials, the Levis two-stroke won many gold medals and was supreme amongst the two-strokes. The 1925 range introduced a

production two-stroke, to be known as the 'Model K', which sported a curved top tube over the petrol tank, giving a much improved appearance and lowered saddle height. The engine was the usual 67 × 70mm 247cc with a cast iron piston, oil pump lubrication (which delivered fresh, cool, clean oil, according to the advertising), internal expanding brakes to both wheels, a three-speed gearbox with chain drive, clutch and kickstarter. Its total weight was only 160lb.

This Model K was a good seller, being offered with a light sidecar and also available as a tradesmans' box outfit. It remained in the catalogue until the end of 1927. A sports edition was introduced in June 1926 and styled 'Model O'. This really was a 'Model K', without the rear carrier, and with a more sporting exhaust pipe. However, these two bikes had to be terminated at the end of 1927, because something special was to be introduced.

As recorded earlier, the little 350cc ohv AJS had proved invincible and Levis must have decided that if you can't beat them, no great harm can be done by joining them! Newey designed a 350cc ohv machine which was to become a classic, but it wasn't a good seller in 1927, the year of its introduction. Everyone was of the opinion that while Levis could make delightful two-stroke machines, a four-stroke was rather a different matter. Newey persevered and for 1928 produced a very quick bike indeed, for the Junior TT. This was ridden by Jack Amott, but the foundry didn't get their sums right because the castings were far too brittle and cylinder after cylinder broke. It was too late to cast replacements and Amott started in the Junior TT knowing that the cylinder would break, which it did on lap one. However, the bike was ready for the Amateur TT in September, and Tim Hunt, who was by far the best amateur rider of the day, was given the job of riding the 350 Levis. Hunt was a certain winner, with the race in his pocket, when on the last lap, at Creg-Ny-Baa, only four miles from the finish, a valve cried enough, and Hunt retired. So near, and yet so far. For the 1929 season, the production 350 had adopted the saddle tank similar to the machine used by Amott and Hunt. Sales however, tended to be slower than anticipated.

Two-stroke development still continued and Newey realised that the stumbling block was the large lump of metal on the piston crown, which was so necessary with the deflector type of piston, but so difficult to keep cool. Scott had the right idea in watercooling the cylinders. Levis had always made beautiful cast-iron pistons, which were only a few thousandths of an inch thick at the skirt but aluminium had to be lighter and

quicker, if only the expansion could be kept under control.

Newey gave this matter a lot of thought and came up with the idea of a transfer port inside the piston. Instead of the mixture passing straight from the crankcase to the cylinder via the transfer port, it was compelled by the special baffle and port in the piston to pass across the underside of the piston crown before it entered the transfer port which should help to cool the piston crown, resulting in a more efficient engine. Two exhaust

Opposite page: G. S. Davidson's 248cc Levis undergoes a pit stop during the 1922 Lightweight TT, which Davidson went on to win. Levis founder Bob Newey is the man filling the fuel tank

Above: one of Levis's most classic machines was the overhead-camshaft 250cc model, introduced in 1933

Below: the two-speed Levis model of 1922 used a 248cc, single-cylinder, two-stroke engine

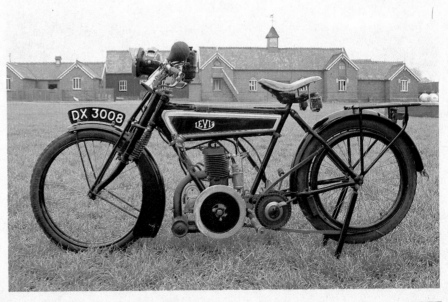

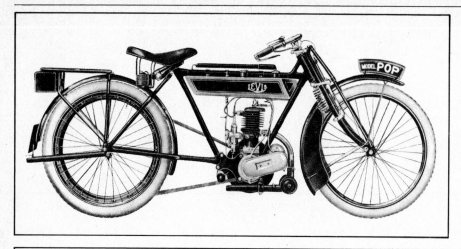

Top: the 211cc, single-cylinder 'Popular' Levis model of 1922

Above: 'the prettiest Levis of all time' was the 350cc A2 model of 1930

Below: first of the Levis four-strokes, the 350cc overhead-valve model A of 1927

Edwards left Levis to join Velocette, he used a similar arrangement to improve the Velocette two-stroke considerably. The 'Sixport' finished at the end of 1930, partly because of piston trouble, but mainly because of the success of the four-stroke models. The normal three-port, 247cc, two-stroke carried on in various types of frame until the early Spring of 1940.

For 1930, the 350cc machine, followed the fashion of the day and grew another exhaust pipe, becoming known as the 'A2'. Everyone considered it to be the prettiest Levis of all time. It was a good performer, being advertised as the 'fastest standard 350', while 'Torrens' of *The Motor Cycle* described it as 'quite the nicest 350' . . . and it sold! The clubman of the period didn't buy a hat if he wanted to get ahead – he bought a Levis, because in those days you bought a bike to ride to work, to compete in trials, take part in grass track racing, or hill climbing – in fact, anything, and this Levis was the 'king pin'. The machine was improved each year, or so we are given to understand, but it got heavier and slower, becoming just another good motor cycle. The quality of Levis motor cycles was always first class, so much so that running-in a new machine was never really necessary, and owners could adjust the handlebars, saddle and footrests through more permutations than on any other machine – they could even adjust the brake pedal too! The Levis works would also alter the specification to suit the customer's preferences.

Owners had a choice of four colours of petrol tanks, different gear ratios, wheel sizes, tyre sizes and cams to give different valve timing – they were even prepared to fit the foot brake pedal on the other

ports and a detachable cylinder head were used for the first time on a Levis two-stroke, christened the 'Sixport'.

On the whole, the machine was good and could have been even better if money had been available to finance its development. It's an ill wind that blows nobody any good, and when Alan

side, if the customer desired. Levis advertising always referred to the bikes as 'a tool-room job!' Certainly one man built one engine. He started with the flywheels and crankcases, and fitted every part until that engine was complete, with payment on an hourly rate. No piece-work of any kind was entertained at Stechford.

The instant success of the 350cc A2 prompted Bob Newey to develop a smaller, 250cc edition, which was a good seller and stayed in the catalogue to the end. Originally, all the bikes had three-speed gearboxes, but eventually four speeds were available as an extra and later, four speeds were standard on

Top: a 1929 247cc two-stroke Levis Sixport model; development of the Sixport, however, was hampered by lack of funds and by 1930 the model was discontinued

Above: the Levis Popular was first introduced in 1911 and did much to establish the lightweight conception of motor cycling. This is a 1916 version and it has a 211cc, air-cooled, single-cylinder engine

both 250 and 350 four-stroke machines. Success with the two ohv models and the decline of the two-stroke market, encouraged the Levis people to develop a 500cc version. This was not as easy as at first throught. A scaled up edition was produced but the performance was pathetic and much midnight oil was burned by Newey and Alan Edwards who altered the cams, valves, port sizes and so on until it was capable of the 80mph target set by the works for a 500.

In 1930, a little 250cc chain-driven ohc AJS had easily won the Lightweight TT. It was ridden by Jimmy Guthrie, who was to achieve fame as a Norton works team rider. The strange thing is that this AJS never contested another TT. It must have impressed Newey, because he designed a very similar ohc unit for Levis. It was introduced late in the 1933 season and offered for sale at £59, which was a lot of money in those dark and dreary Depressed days.

Enthusiasts could buy a 500 Norton Model 18 at exactly the same price, which proves that the general public prefer quantity to quality. The standard ohv Norton in 1934 was fairly mundane while the little 'cammy' Levis was a jewel. After about two years in the catalogue it was withdrawn. The machine was a real classic and only one is known to have survived.

Around 1936, Ray Mason joined

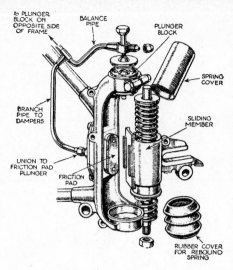

Above: the oil damped spring frame used on the 1939 350 and 500cc Levis models. In the Levis design – the work of R. W. Mason – the two plungers were balanced and damped hydraulically. A feature of the system was that it provided automatic compensation for the weight of the rider and passenger

Below: this is one of the models on which R. W. Mason's spring frame was used. It is a 1939 Levis roadster, powered by a side-valve engine of 350cc

Levis and together with Bob Newey, he designed the big 82 × 112mm Levis 600 single. This had a cradle frame and was a winner from the beginning. The only trouble was that the gearbox fitted to the 1937 models was not up to the power developed, but a heavier gearbox introduced for 1938 cured that problem. This must have been the best 600cc single cylinder machine ever produced, in any quantity, in this country. Ray Mason developed a couple of special 600's and one, ridden by Bob Foster, thrilled the crowds at 'Red Marley' hill climb for many years.

At the end of 1938, Ray Mason designed an oil damped spring frame to be fitted as an option on the 350 and 500cc machines, and if World War II hadn't intervened, we should have heard much more of this idea. For good measure, Mason also designed a very lively 350cc side valve Levis, which must have been a winner if only production could have been continued, but wartime measures put Levis on to work of national importance – making air compressors – which they continue to make to the present day.

Recently, the company has changed its name to Leviss, just to prove to some foreign countries that they have no religious bias, and also to avoid confusion with that well known manufacturer of denim clothing.   RHP

This magnificent four-color encyclopedia is brought to you by Columbia House
in cooperation with Orbis Publishing Ltd., one of Great Britain's most enterprising publishers.
Rather than change any of the encyclopedia's authoritative international automotive text, we have
included a glossary of terms that will give you immediate American equivalents, and conversion tables
for the international metric system.

Glossary

BRITISH	AMERICAN
Aerial	Antenna
Aero engine	Aircraft engine
Aerofoil	Airfoil
Aluminium	Aluminum
Anti-froth baffle	Tank baffle
Anti-knock rating	Octane rating
Apron	Skirt
Back-to-front	Backwards
Back to square one	Start over from the beginning
Badge engineering	Identical bikes with different nameplates (such as the BSA and Triumph brands)
Bang on	Exactly
Benzol	Benzene
Big-end	Larger (crankshaft) end of a connecting rod
Bi-metal	Bi-metallic
Blow-back	Backfire in the intake manifold or carburetor
Blower	Supercharger
Bottle-screw jack	Type of hydraulic jack
Box spanner	Socket
Brake horsepower (bhp)	Net horsepower (hp)
Brake servo	Power brake
Bush	Bushing
Capacity	Displacement
Carburettor	Carburetor
Carcass	Tire body or plies
Castellated nut	Castle nut
Chain wheel	Sprocket
Choke flap	Choke plate
Clutch release bearing	Clutch throwout bearing
Cogged belt	Rubber timing belt
Collets	Split collar retainers
Conrod	Connecting rod
Control box	Voltage regulator
Core plug	Freeze-out or Welsh plug
Crash box	Non-synchromesh transmission
Crocodile clip	Alligator clip
Crown wheel	Ring gear
Damper	Shock absorber
Decarbonise	Remove carbon deposits from combustion chamber
De-clutch	Disengage clutch
Decoke	See "Decarbonise"
De-ionised water	Distilled water
Detonation	Pre-ignition
Dipped headlight	Low beam
Dipswitch	High/low beam switch
Directly	Right away
DOE test	A state inspection

BRITISH	AMERICAN
Double knocker	Double overhead camshaft
Downdraught	Downdraft
Dustbin	Garbage can
Dust excluder	Seal
Dynamo	Generator
Earth	Electrical ground
Earthing strip	Ground wire
East-west mounting	Transverse mounting
End-float	Runout
Epicyclic gearbox	Planitary transmission
Estate car	Station wagon
Extreme-pressure lubricant	Heavy duty (gear) oil
Farrier	Blacksmith, horse shoer
First-motion shaft	Input shaft
Fit	Install
Flat-out	Top speed
Fore-and-aft mounting	Longitudinal mounting
40 years on	40 years in the future
Gaiter	Rubber boot
Gearbox	Transmission
Gearchange	Shift pedal or lever (n.) or shift (v.)
Glassfibre	Fiberglass
Glass-reinforced plastic	Fiberglass
Gudgeon pin	Piston or wrist pin
Half-liners	Split shell bearings
Half shaft	Axle shaft
High tension	High voltage
High-tension leads	Spark plug cables
Hose clip	Hose clamp
Ignition harness	Ignition cable set
Immediately	As soon as
Indicators	Turn signals
Induction	Intake
Inlet	Intake
Jubilee clip	Brand of worm-drive hose clamp
Judder	Shudder
Jump leads	Jumper cables or wire
Just on	Exactly
Kerb	Curb
Knife cuts	Tire sipes
Layshaft	Countershaft
Leads	Cables or wires
Low-tension	Low voltage
Main beam	High headlight beam, "brights"
Marque	Brand, make
Midlands	English industrial center
Mileage recorder	Odometer

Glossary

BRITISH	AMERICAN
Mileometer	Odometer
Mixture	Fuel-air mixture
Monobloc	Engine with crankcase and cylinder block cast in one piece
Monocoque	Frame constructed of sheetmetal box sections rather than tubes
Motor	Engine
Nave plate	Wheel cover, hubcap
Nil	Zero, nothing
Non-return valve	One-way valve
Number plate	License plate
One-lunger	Single-cylinder
One-off	One-of-a-kind
ONO	"Or near offer" (used in classified ads)
Opposite number	Equal, equivalent, mate
Overrun	Coasting in gear
Paraffin	Kerosene
Perspex	Plexiglas
Petroil	Gas and oil mixture
Petrol	Gasoline
Petrol pump	Fuel pump
Pillion	Passenger saddle or seat
Pinking	Pinging
Plunger	Detent ball
Pocketing	Excess valve seat wear
Pots	Cylinders
Production	Stock
Prop stand	Kick stand
Propeller shaft	Driveshaft
Purpose-built	Special
Quietening ramps	Low acceleration cam profile for quiet engine operation
RAC	Royal Automobile Club
Rear lamp	Tail light
Retrograde step	Step backwards
Rev counter	Tachometer
Ring spanner	Box wrench
Road roar	Tire noise
Rocker	Rocker arm
Rocker box	Rocker or valve cover
Rocker clearance	Valve clearance
Round	Around
Rubber solution	Rubber cement
Running-in	Break in
Running-on	Dieseling
Saloon	Sedan
Scheme	Plan, program
Screen	Windshield
Scuttle	Cowl

BRITISH	AMERICAN
Second-motion shaft	Countershaft
Sediment chamber	Trap
Self-locking nut	Locknut
Servo assisted	Power assisted
Shunt	Accident, bump, crash
Side-draught	Side draft
Side-valve engine	Flathead engine
Slow-running	Idle
Small-end	Smaller (piston) end of a connecting rod
Snap-in valve	Tubeless tire valve
Spade connector	Bayonet connector
Spanner	Wrench
Spigot	Pin
Spit-back	See "blow-back"
Split cones	Split collar retainers
Spot-on	Exactly
Squib	Auto seatback
5 star petrol	100 octane gasoline
4 star petrol	99-97 octane gasoline
3 star petrol	96-94 octane gasoline
2 star petrol	93-90 octane gasoline
Starting handle	Crank
Strangler flap	Choke plate
Sump	Oil pan
Swivel pin	Kingpin
Tab washer	Lock washer
Third-motion shaft	Output shaft
Throttle-stop screw	Idle speed screw
Throttle valve	Butterfly valve
Tick-over	Idle speed
Tin	Can
Tommy bar	Breaker bar, socket wrench
Top end	Cylinder head, or top speed
Trafficators	Early brand of turn signals
Twin-choke carburettor	Two-barrel carburetor
Tyre	Tire
Undo	Remove
Unsymmetrical	Asymmetrical
Venturi	Carburetor barrel
Volume-control screw	Idle mixture screw
Wheel brace	Lug wrench
Windscreen	Windshield
Wing	Fender
Wire wool	Steel wool
Works	Factory
Zinc-oxide grease	Bearing grease

Metric Equivalents
(Based on National Bureau of Standards)

Length

Centimeter (Cm.)	= 0.3937 in.	In.	= 2.5400 cm.
Meter (M.)	= 3.2808 ft.	Ft.	= 0.3048 m.
Meter	= 1.0936 yd.	Yd.	= 0.9144 m.
Kilometer (Km.)	= 0.6214 mile	Mile	= 1.6093 km.

Area

Sq. cm.	= 0.1550 sq. in.	Sq. in.	= 6.4516 sq. cm.
Sq. m.	= 10. 7639 sq. ft.	Sq. ft.	= 0.0929 sq. m.
Sq. m.	= 1.1960 sq. yd.	Sq. yd.	= 0.8361 sq. m.
Hectare	= 2.4710 acres	Acre	= 0.4047 hectare
Sq. km.	= 0.3861 sq. mile	Sq. mile	= 2.5900 sq. km.

Volume

Cu. cm.	= 0.0610 cu. in.	Cu. in.	= 16.3872 cu. cm.
Cu. m.	= 35.3145 cu. ft.	Cu. ft.	= 0.0283 cu. m.
Cu. m.	= 1.3079 cu. yd.	Cu. yd.	= 0.7646 cu. m.

Capacity

Liter	= 61.0250 cu. in	Cu. in.	= 0.0164 liter
Liter	= 0.0353 cu. ft.	Cu. ft.	= 28.3162 liters
Liter	= 0.2642 gal. (U.S.)	Gal.	= 3.7853 liters
Liter	= 0.0284 bu. (U.S.)	Bu.	= 35.2383 liters

Liter = $\begin{cases} 1000.027 \text{ cu. cm.} \\ 1.0567 \text{ qt. (liquid) or } 0.9081 \text{ qt. (dry)} \\ 2.2046 \text{ lb. of pure water at 4 C} = 1 \text{ kg.} \end{cases}$

Weight

Gram. (Gm.)	= 15.4324 grains	Grain	= 0.0648 gm.
Gram	= 0.0353 oz.	Oz.	= 28.3495 gm.
Kilogram (Kg.)	= 2.2046 lb.	Lb.	= 0.4536 kg.
Kg.	= 0.0011 ton (sht.)	Ton (sht.)	= 907.1848 kg.
Ton (met.)	= 1.1023 ton (sht.)	Ton (sht.)	= 0.9072 ton (met.)
Ton (met.)	= 0.9842 ton (lg.)	Ton (lg.)	= 1.0160 ton (met.)

Pressure

1 kg. per sq. cm.   = 14.223 lb. per sq. in.
1 lb. per sq. in.   = 0.0703 kg. per sq. cm.
1 kg. per sq. m.   = 0.2048 lb. per sq. ft.
1 lb. per sq. ft.   = 4.8824 kg. per sq. m.
1 kg. per sq. cm.   = 0.9678 normal atmosphere

1 normal atmosphere = $\begin{cases} 1.0332 \text{ kg. per sq. cm.} \\ 1.0133 \text{ bars} \\ 14.696 \text{ lb. per sq. in.} \end{cases}$

How to Convert Metric Measurements to U.S. Equivalents

TO CONVERT:	TO:	MULTIPLY BY EXACTLY:	MULTIPLY BY APPROXIMATELY
Millimeters (mm)	Inches (in.)	0.039	4/100
Centimeters (cm)	Inches (in.)	0.394	4/10
Meters (m)	Feet (ft.)	3.28	3¼
Meters (m)	Yards (yd.)	1.09	1-1/10
Kilometers (km)	Miles (mi.)	0.621	⅝
Kilometers per hour (kph)	Miles per hour (mph)	0.621	⅝
Kilometers per liter (kpl)	Miles per gallon (mpg)	2.352	2⅜
Square centimeters (cm²)	Square inches (sq. in.)	0.155	3/20
Square meters (m²)	Square feet (sq. ft.)	10.8	11
Square meters (m²)	Square yards (sq. yds.)	1.2	1¼
Cubic centimeters (cc)	Cubic inches (c. i.)	0.061	1/16
Liters (1000cc)	Cubic inches (c. i.)	61.025	61
Cubic meters (m³)	Cubic feet (cu. ft.)	35.3	35⅓
Cubic meters (m³)	Cubic yards (cu. yds.)	1.31	1⅓
Liters (l)	Pints (pt.)	2.11	2-1/10
Liters (l)	Quarts (qt.)	1.06	10/9
Liters (l)	U.S. gallons (gal.)	0.264	¼
Liters (l)	Imperial gallons	0.22	2/9
Imperial gallons	U.S. gallons	1.2	1¼
Miles per Imperial gallon	Miles per U.S. gallon	1.2	1¼
Grams (gm)	Ounces (oz.)	0.035	3/100
Kilograms (kg)	Pounds (lb.)	2.2	2¼
Metric tons	Tons	1.1	11/10
Hundredweight (cwt.)	Pounds (lb.)	112.0	—
Stone	Pounds (lb.)	14.0	—
Kilogram-meters (kg-m)	Foot-pounds (ft.-lb.)	7.232	7¼
Kilograms per square centimeter	Pounds per square inch (psi)	14.22	14¼
Metric horsepower (bhp DIN)	U.S. horsepower	0.9859	—

How to Convert U.S. Measurements to Metric Equivalents

TO CONVERT:	TO:	MULTIPLY BY EXACTLY:	MULTIPLY BY APPROXIMATELY
Inches (in.)	Millimeters (mm)	25.4	25½
Inches (in.)	Centimeters (cm)	2.54	2½
Feet (ft.)	Meters (m)	0.305	3/10
Yards (yd.)	Meters (m)	0.914	9/10
Miles (mi.)	Kilometers (km)	1.609	8/5
Miles per hour (mph)	Kilometers per hour (kph)	1.609	8/5
Miles per gallon (mpg)	Kilometers per liter (kpl)	0.425	2/5
Square inches (sq. in.)	Square centimeters (cm²)	6.45	6½
Square feet (sq. ft.)	Square meters (m²)	0.093	1/10
Square yards (sq. yd.)	Square meters (m²)	0.836	4/5
Cubic inches (c. i.)	Cubic centimeters (cc)	16.4	16½
Cubic inches (c. i.)	Liters (1000cc)	0.164	4/25
Cubic feet (cu. ft.)	Cubic meters (m³)	0.0283	3/100
Cubic yards (cu. yd.)	Cubic meters (m³)	0.765	¾
Pints (pt.)	Liters (l)	0.473	½
Quarts (qt.)	Liters (l)	0.946	9/10
U.S. gallons (gal.)	Liters (l)	3.78	3¾
Imperial gallons (gal.)	Liters (l)	4.55	4½
Ounces (oz.)	Grams (gm)	28.4	28½
Pounds (lb.)	Grams (gm)	454.0	450
Pounds (lb.)	Kilograms (kg)	0.454	½
Foot-pounds (ft.-lb.)	Kilogram-meters (kg-m)	0.1383	3/20
Pounds per square inch (psi)	Kilograms per square cm	0.0703	7/100
U.S. horsepower	Metric horsepower (bhp DIN)	1.014	—